A HISTORY
of
FISHING
— IN THE —
FLORIDA KEYS

ANGLER'S PARADISE

BOB T. EPSTEIN

Charleston ⊢H⊣ London
THE
History
PRESS

Commerce and travel to the Keys before the advent of the motor—the sailboat. *Courtesy of J. Wilkinson, president of the Keys Historical Trust.*

Published by The History Press
Charleston, SC 29403
www.historypress.net

Cover image of Ernest Hemingway is courtesy of the Ernest Hemingway Collection, John F. Kennedy Presidential Library and Museum, Boston.

First published 2013

Manufactured in the United States

ISBN 978.1.60949.998.3

Library of Congress CIP data applied for.

Contents

Preface   7
Acknowledgements   9
Introduction   13

1. Most Common Game Fish of the Florida Keys   29
2. Indigenous People and Indian Key   55
3. Fishing Methods and Travels to the Keys   65
4. Fishing Guides and Their Exploits   69
5. Private and Governmental Programs   73
6. A Special Captain and a Unique Lifelong Fossil Hunter   77
7. Fish Preparation, Recipes and Preservation   81
8. The Ubiquitous Key Lime Pie and Famous Florida Lobster   83
9. Industrial Art in Fishing Rods over the Past 120 Years   87
10. Bud N' Mary's Fishing Marina and My Fishing Experiences   91
11. Hemingway, Mel Fisher and Celebrity Anglers'
    Influences in Key West   105
12. FADs, Wrecked or Sunken Ships, Immigrant Dolphin
    Tactics and Mangroves   111
13. The Old and the New Seven-Mile Bridge and
    Keys Lighthouses   121
14. Outdoor Writers and a Marathon History   127

CONTENTS

15. Conservation, Geologic and Archaeological Features,
    Sea Turtles and Sharks   135
16. A Florida Keys Timeline and Notes about
    Long Key and Marathon   151

Sources   165
Index   167
About the Author   171

Preface

This book is dedicated to all the fishing guides and offshore captains who have shown me the adventures of the Gulf Stream, oceans, rivers, streams, lakes, ponds, the Caribbean and the Gulf of Mexico in pursuit of the finny creatures that make their homes there. Thank you, all! The many hundreds of guides and captains who made it possible for me to publish more than 2,400 fishing articles just cannot all be mentioned—that would take another book.

Fishing has the elements of religion's highest function: faith. Faith that no matter what in the world we do, if all the right thoughts, actions and considerations of God, nature and others are met, a person can expect the highest of rewards. This belief plays out in every moment of every day in one's life, especially if one has such faith and patience as a fisherman and a lifelong desire to also be a fisher of men.

As this is a history of fishing in the Keys and I have often been asked, when I offer lectures about fishing at various venues, "Who invented fishing?" I would be remiss in not stating what I have learned over the years that addresses that question. From all evidence, based on cave drawings, fossils, early dated shell hooks, gorges, spears, stone tools, arrowheads and other such artifacts, it appears that people fished over 100,000 years ago. Early peoples fished with their hands (an early form of today's so-called noodling), poisons, hand lines, gorges, spears, traps and nets. Thirty thousand years ago, Pacific Islanders first fished in salt water. Egyptian records show that in 2000 BC, people fished for food; records

The author always thrills to a bonefish catch and celebrates it with a very wet release. *Photo by author.*

in hieroglyphics show that about 1400 BC, Egyptians fished for pleasure, as evidenced in rods being used by those of rank in their society. They used small bronze hooks, some sort of artificial flies, woven plant fiber and horsehair lines. However, any definitive treatise is nearly impossible to ascertain, as the human being is generally far more inventive then even he gives himself credit for. I suspect it would take a library of books and writings to even partially address the true history of fishing and who actually invented the sport, which would probably be impossible. The true answers to this question shall remain shrouded in history, never to be learned, just conjectured and mused over with a short, curved smile on the lips.

Acknowledgements

This book, like my seven other labors of love, would not have been possible without the enthusiastic assistance of several folks. These friends and acquaintances were excited to be part of the process of creating this book. First and foremost, and of highly special note in making this book a reality, is my wife, Barbara. For half a century, she has been my most enthusiastic supporter and the one person who has been able to keep me out of the procrastinators' club. Frankly, everyone I mention in these acknowledgements has helped make it possible for me to complete this informative and fun book project.

Stu Apte, a retired commercial pilot, writer and author, is a fishing world record holder and guide to the rich and famous (and us guys and gals, too). He offered images for this book. Mark Sosin, a true and tried outdoor writer, filmmaker, one of my great writing mentors and a major player in the Fishing Hall of Fame, offered his early recollections of fishing in the Keys. Islamorada residents Keys historian Irving R. Eyster, his wife Jeanne and their daughter Barbara Edgar offered a large amount of input through Irving's book *Islamorada and More*, along with their archive of images acquired over a lifetime of education, teaching and studying the Florida Keys. Keys historian Jerry Wilkinson also had a fine image archive for me to use. Monte Green, a pal always wanting to take me fishing, as well as Mike Puto, an excellent friend and the mayor emeritus of Marathon, offered input and assistance. Enthusiastic Puto assisted with images and great information about all things Marathon, the Seven-Mile Bridge and historical Pigeon

Key. Thank you to the International Game Fish Association (IGFA) E.K. Harry Library for wonderful early images and reference books on all things fishy. Thanks also to Al Degraff and Harry Dillon, who took me on my first fishing trip when I arrived in the Keys more than thirty-seven years ago and many more fishing trips to follow. Thanks to Richard and his brother, Scott Stanczyk, who fished me from the Keys to Mexico, showing me really big game fishing at its best. Richard took me bonefishing several times a week, poling my butt to some fantastic bonefish catches, including one that probably was a world record of a seventeen-plus pounder on eight-pound test. We took just one photo, measured it and then released it. It certainly left me with a thrill-of-a-lifetime memory. That image is in this book, too. Additionally, I thank Richard for introducing me to tarpon fishing. I appreciated his patience on the night when a huge tarpon dragged our boat around for three hours until I could hardly stand the pain. My arm and wrist were pain-bent until the tarpon mercifully let me go.

Also, thanks to the other guides and captains who availed me of their boats and expertise, such as the captain on the *Kalex* and Captain Randy Towe, who early on assisted me greatly in obtaining fishing photos for my articles and taught me quite a bit about fishing for various backcountry species. Thanks to Captain Rufus Wakeman, a dedicated angler and gentleman, who took me fishing and taught me what to use so I would never get seasick again. Thanks to guide Ken Knudssen, who took me along when his young daughter fought the "big ones" and gave new meaning to how great father-daughter quality time can be. Thank you Paul Chaffee, my "Blood Brother"—you have always been my friend and showed me all those fishing times on the Connecticut River.

I know I have failed to mention so many others who have increased my knowledge of fishing, especially in the Keys and its incredible fishing opportunities. Also, to so many others who have contributed to my experiences in the Keys and fishing all over the world, I apologize, but I know it would take another book to include you all, and you are all a factor in my continuing love of this ever-challenging, delightful sport!

There are always several time-consuming steps in putting together a book from scratch. I want to thank the folks at The History Press for all their excellent editing time and for handling the various jobs that make a book a worthwhile effort that anyone and everyone would want to read. My mother, Mary, and my father, Nat, have also been an inspiration and cheerleaders for all my projects, as are my uncle Bill and aunt Rose Brenner. Bill, a successful inventor and engineer, has always given me first-class advice; on the few

Lady of the ladder. This angler caught a fish bigger than she is. Tarpon are the main action game fish today, as they were in the days of yore in the Keys. *Courtesy of IGFA.*

occasions when I didn't listen to him, I wish I had! Also, thanks to Dennis Raynor, my earliest fishing friend, who fished alongside me in Long Island all those years ago, the memory of which is now painted in happy, pastel images in my mind. To all my teachers and professors in my school years who encouraged me to become a writer, I salute you everywhere in life and in heaven. Of special note is my grandfather David Schwartz, who instilled in me his love of all things fishing and left his legacy for me to always pursue the memories of those times and places first experienced in my youth in Upstate New York. Those were times of wonderment. I cherish memories of those pickerel, bass, perch and trout that I lusted after before and since his passing in 1959, continuing on where he left off, always trying to find that fishing Valhalla where the big ones played and sometimes being there in that heaven-on-earth when they wanted to play with me, too!

I certainly would be remiss in not mentioning my sons, David and Brian, my true fishing buddies from even before the time they could hold a rod. When we all moved from Vermont fishing in the Connecticut River and its many tributaries to the Florida Keys Gulf Stream and the Gulf of Mexico backcountry, we fished in our towered, twenty-two-foot Mako, semi-displacement hull boat (the boat went anywhere, shallow or deep), ranging far and wide looking for marlin. Yes, we did find them, and we did catch a few, too. However, I do want to apologize to them for yelling each time they got so excited when we saw marlin behind the boat that they fumbled lines and baits and the marlin swam away. I yelled at them and now wish I hadn't. Sorry guys, and thank goodness I didn't turn you off from fishing because of it. But you did know how excited Pop got when the big ones were behind the boat!

I have fished with the rich and famous, and I have fished with so many others not rich and famous. I have fished and talked fishing with presidents and generals such as George W. Bush and General Norman Schwarzkopf and fished with and became fast friends with Curt Gowdy, of World Wide Sportsman fame. I spent quiet, quality time with baseball legend Ted Williams; Florida senators and congressmen; directors of fishing tournaments; business magnates in trucking, plastics (Dick Jacobs of Dayton, Ohio), the petroleum industry and the arts (Guy Harvey); and world record holder Billy Pate, now gone to that big tarpon hole in the sky, and found one common denominator for us all: fishing levels the playing field of life. All men truly are created equal in their joy and delight of their personal piscatorial endeavors and their thoughts of their own individualized experiences. The world's problems shrink and melt away from one's mind while fishing, making all things peaceful or exciting, strictly based on the kind of fish one focuses on. Being hooked up to any of the fish mentioned in this book will give no man or woman pause to think negatively of his or her lot in life and any of his or her daily troubles and anxieties. There is only room for the thoughts: will the hook hold, the reels seize up, the wrist and arm fail or the line or rod break? These feelings and the exhilaration of how life should be unwind, or wind, like the smoothest finely tuned reel spool. This is our monumental reward.

Introduction

Today, if you follow the sun down south through Florida from the northernmost reaches of either the West or East Coast, you will, after several hundred miles, begin a journey down U.S. 1 from the city of Homestead 150 miles toward the end of the Keys' tail of Florida in Key West. You will be driving on the Overseas Highway. For many miles, the drive is truly overseas.

When discussing fishing in the Keys, I must take into account that there is more to discuss than just the finned and gilled ones. Men fished for sunken treasures, for turtles, crustaceans and mollusks, warm-blooded animals like the manatee, living jewels for aquarium tanks, coral, sponges, conch shells filled with tasty meaty conchs, shrimps and a wide variety of both game fish and food fish.

Not long after Christopher Columbus reached the New World in 1492, adventurer Ponce de León and fellow Spanish chronicler Antonio de Herrera set sail toward Florida in search of the elusive Fountain of Youth. They never found the fountain, but they did find the Florida Keys in 1513 and its surrounding habitats, where billions of fish and untold numbers of invertebrate sea animals lived. The following is precisely what Herrera wrote for posterity in his *Tales of Old Florida*:

> *To all this line of islands and rock islets they gave the name of Los Martires* [The Martyrs] *because, seen from a distance, the rocks as they rose to view appeared like men who were suffering; and the name remained fitting because of the many that have been lost there since.*

The legendary fishing outdoor writer and author Zane Grey with four sailfish he captured on his Von Hofe reel and bamboo rod. This image was taken at the Long Key Fishing Club that Grey helped develop and made famous. *Courtesy of J. Wilkinson, president of the Keys Historical Trust.*

Today, over five hundred years later, more than three million visitors, from all corners of the earth, come each year to the Florida Keys, which stretch out in a scimitar-like, curved necklace of rough and uncut diamonds. These few islands, from Key Largo to Key West, out of more than 1,700 other islands, are cobbled together by forty-three bridges, and visitors come by air, boat and auto. These tourists make pilgrimages to the Florida Keys mainly to fish—and it's no wonder, with more than six hundred fish varieties in Florida waters, most of which are caught in the waters between Miami and the 198 miles from Miami down to Key West. Tourists come to view or catch fish and other marine life, such as Florida lobster in their season, contributing up to $1.2 billion to the economy of the Florida Keys. In years gone by, there was very little pressure on the fish of the Keys; there just weren't that many people fishing for them. Today, the Keys are based on a tourism economy, no longer a commercial fishery economy.

According to the writings of author Zane Grey (an outdoor magazine writer, adventure book author and world-famous angler), the waters between Indian Key and Bahia Honda Harbor were the very best in the

Above: A nearly fourteen-pound bonefish caught in Islamorada waters in the 1950s. *Courtesy of Irving Eyster.*

Left: In 1916, catching a sailfish on a fly rod was considered a great sporting achievement. The man holding the rod is dressed in sporting attire, as it was the dress code of a true sportsman of the day. *Courtesy of IGFA.*

world (as he wrote in the 1920s). So today, it's no wonder that—thanks to locals, visitors from all over the United States and foreigners who come to duel with offshore fish such as swordfish, marlin, sailfish, mackerel, tuna, wahoo and dolphin (mahi-mahi)—there are fewer and smaller fish than in the past. Yet fortunately there is still a large assortment of them, especially the aforementioned pelagics. There is also abundant inshore flats fishing for bonefish, tarpon, permit, redfish, snook and sea trout, for which the Keys are most noted. Without a doubt, the true magnetic draw to these bony islands is these underwater finned residents. If you ask anyone about the Florida Keys, most responses are about fishing, Key Lime pie (sort of the "apple pie" of South Florida), fun in the sun, seafood and fish houses, as well as diving and snorkeling.

Early visits to the Keys during the 1800s and up to the time when Flagler strung those aforementioned rugged uncut diamonds together with train tracks and bridges, fewer than two hundred folks north of the Keys ventured south to fish in an entire year. Besides it being a major adventure for travelers to get to the Keys and stay there, they had billions of mosquitoes to contend with before the invention of Deet. (I will add that I believe the mosquitoes would have eaten Deet then, too!) It was a major adventure by sailboat, and all supplies had to be brought in, not bought or procured in the Keys. The first housewife settler—a Mrs. Mary Ann Russell—who came from the Bahamas around 1834 with her husband, Richard, to settle on 162 acres, stated that "the main trouble living in the Keys had been trying to keep the bear and panther out of her garden." It was, like so much of Florida in those times, wild country.

Flagler's railroad was completed all the way to Key West in 1912. Then, in 1926, construction began on the Overseas Highway, and road bridges changed the access. The Keys would never again be a sleepy, out-of-the-way, jungle-like, remote, untouched tropical paradise again. However, when the Labor Day hurricane struck the Keys in 1935, it forever changed the way visitors traveled to the various sparsely distributed areas such as homes, mom and pop cottages, little hotels, motels, auto courts and, eventually, resorts that sprang up to service the visiting anglers. After the Great Depression, which severely impacted most Americans, the roadway to Key West was completed. In 1938, the Keys were still experiencing hard times like most of the United States. At least no one froze to death, and grits, grunts and lobster tails kept locals in "vittles."

One thing is for sure, the Florida Keys are like a river—ever changing, never static, always flowing inevitably toward modernity. From the time they

Above: A swordfish catch on the *Catch 22* charter boat, captained by Scott Stanczyk. The fish was caught by Captain Nick Stanczyk (far left), Scott's nephew. The fish weighed in at well over five hundred pounds. A whole large squid was the bait. *Courtesy of Captain Nick Stanczyk.*

Left: Henry Flagler at the caboose end of his train on its maiden voyage to Key West. *Courtesy of J. Wilkinson, president of the Keys Historical Trust.*

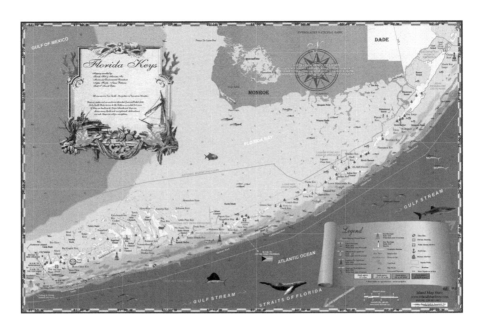

This modern Florida Keys map names all the Keys islands, both attached by the forty-three bridges and those that must be reached by boat. All the Keys islands with bridges have residents, and only some of the out-islands have private and governmental owners. The Keys island locations and Overseas Highway are delineated by mile markers. MM-150 begins after coming onto the eighteen-mile stretch through the Everglades and ends at MM-0 in Key West at the marker that says, "90 miles to Cuba." *Courtesy of Island Map Store. com, Terrell, Hall & Associates, www.Islandmapstore.com.*

were jungle, when untamed pumas, bears and snakes abounded and a man could be made mad by mosquitoes (much like what happened when the Panama Canal was cut through the jungle, where the smallest inhabitants inflicted the greatest misery and death on the interlopers working the canal), the Keys were finally conquered (temporarily) for the use of man.

Modern-day visitors directly support hundreds of flats, backcountry, inshore, big-water charter boat captains and mates. Visitors take advantage of the diving, snorkeling, sailing, fishing, dive shops, bait and tackle shops, marinas, restaurants, hotels, motels and campgrounds. Almost all of the multitude of businesses, from automotive to carpet, tile, carpentry, plumbing and electric companies, to name a few, are supported by locals and visitors, too.

Commercial fishing is the second-largest industry in the Keys. Some of the most important commercial species are spiny lobster, stone crab claws (only eaten in recent history), pink shrimp, mackerel, grouper, sea trout and snapper. However, the grouper, sea trout and snapper declined in availability as they were so heavily fished. Most grouper at restaurants is now brought in frozen from South America and other countries. Collectors of tropical fish and other marine life also profit from the reef environment (but now there are major regulations throughout the Keys on taking saltwater species for aquariums). The commercial fleet supported about 1,200 families, as of 2006, which was close to 5 percent of Monroe County's population. Stock Island alone lands seven million pounds, with a dockside value of $24 million—that's 5 percent of Florida's total landings and 13 percent of its total value. In 2006, Monroe County was ranked the fifth most valuable port in the nation, with a dockside value of about $54.4 million. This figure does not include retail sales and profits made by wholesalers who market seafood products worldwide. It's reasonable to predict that seafood and related industries earned upwards of $70 million. This does not take into account the millions of dollars of shrimp caught off Key West and landed at other ports around the Gulf of Mexico. However, it is reasonable to assume that fish and seafood dollars are declining in direct proportion to their overfishing today. (The data information used here is partially attributed to National Marine Sanctuary information as of a 2006 census.)

Down through the history of the Keys, there have been several different fishing enterprises in and around Keys waters, along with the pineapples, barrels of limes, tomato farms and, in Key West, tobacco in the form of cigars (yes, an agricultural product, but in today's law, all other commercial fishing in the form of actual farming of fish is under the jurisdiction of the U.S. Agricultural Department).

Besides the mackerel fishery, there was a busy turtle-harvesting industry, a sponge-gathering industry, shrimping, lobster, bottom ground fish trapping for snapper and grouper, conch meat and shell. In Big Pine Key, there was a factory that harvested and shipped to New Jersey sharkskin for shagreen, a tough sharkskin leather, and shark fins for the Asian trade. Also, the aforementioned coral and tropical fish harvesting for the aquarium trade was going strong. One industry not known by many was quarrying for old reef stone. "Keystone" was mined and cut for building facings and other architectural needs.

The evolution from harvesting natural resources to tourists from around the world viewing these resources by diving, snorkeling and leaving few footprints, taking images of what once was a free-for-all for anything that could be sold or traded, is giving the Keys a breather of sorts for regeneration,

but only because of laws that govern the use of these resources. Today, the Keys are finally getting a sewage system that could help stop some of the pollution of the living reefs and water tables.

Today, the sponge industry in the Keys is gone. The tobacco cigar rollers' descendants hawk Chinese trinkets on Duval Street. The turtle is a protected species and no longer on the menu in Florida restaurants, and those harvesting and selling its shell and byproducts are subject to fine and imprisonment. The pineapples are gone, with Hawaii taking over that industry. The National Marine Sanctuary has put a stop to harvesting coral and the little colorful fish that lived around and amongst this natural treasure, with several large areas totally off limits to any kind of fishing and harvesting. The once prolific conch shells are now imported from the Philippines. Shells from another era of bounty are now seen as walkway gravel piled high at many docks in the Bahamas. A few piles are still to be crushed for walkways in the Keys. Today, there is a conch farm in the Cayman Islands. It does sell conch for reseeding and meats, but the conch (the cow of the sea is an herbivore) takes a minimum of five years to mature to a harvestable size.

Inshore, there is an entire hierarchy of fish royalty, from the bonefish, tarpon and permit, the triage of the perfecta, to the fabulous fighting snook, sea trout, excellent tasting mangrove snapper and the coarse, easily caught redfish. These fish and others today (as in the past hundred years) attract anglers to both shore and kayak fishing, and hundreds of fishing guides and their skiffs are hired in pursuit of these fish for picture trophies and the plate as well. Today, with forty-three bridges that connect each of the Keys Islands, bridge fishing is also a great draw for anglers without boats. They bring their families and friends to go out to sea without ever getting their sneakers wet and still catch fish, too. It wasn't always this way.

Opposite, top: Shrimp boats pack the harbor in Key West—a major commercial fishery, although this fishery today is greatly reduced in size due mainly to overfishing. *Courtesy of J. Wilkinson, president of the Keys Historical Trust.*

Opposite, bottom: This small sailboat delivers and picks up various agricultural goods. Noting that most Keys waters are very shallow near shore, it was common practice for early settlers to use a horse and wagon for these pickups and deliveries. *Courtesy of J. Wilkinson, president of the Keys Historical Trust.*

A sponge sailing craft festooned with necklaces of these hard-won invertebrate animals. The sponge fishing industry was very active in the Keys, but like everything else that has been overfished, today sponging is basically a dead industry in Florida waters, since modern sponges are created from various synthetic materials. *Courtesy of J. Wilkinson, president of the Keys Historical Trust.*

No Name Key Old Wooden Bridge was replaced over thirty years ago. Today, it's made of concrete, and this bridge is still used as a fishing bridge. It probably has the least amount of traffic of all Keys bridges, as it leads only to No Name Key, well off the Overseas Highway main thoroughfare. *Courtesy of J. Wilkinson, president of the Keys Historical Trust.*

Redfish were called channel bass in the 1800s. They were thick in many of the cuts and rivers, especially in the Indian River and lagoons. Anglers of the day who made their way to South Florida thought nothing of loading hundreds of pounds of fish (any fish were fair game). There was no thought or care about releasing fish; they were gaffed and loaded into canoes and sailing craft, later to be displayed as proof of the angler's prowess and success—his bragging rights over a glass of port at the hotel or on the sailboat.

The following account from an 1889 *Outing* magazine column titled "Winter's Sport in Florida," by O.A. Mygatt, is from a New York angler who came by train to fish South Florida and the Keys in the late 1800s. Mike and his friend from New York wanted to escape the snow and slush during late winter 1889:

> We packed up our rods and gear and headed for Jacksonville, Florida for a 6-week sojourn in Florida. Tuesday saw us at Rockledge on the Indian River, bargaining for a sailboat and two row boats. That same afternoon, we laid in a supply of provisions; flower [sic] eggs and canned goods. Our skipper with a genial well posted attitude Mr. MacGruger, and good natured Peter acted as cook and aide-de-camp. We headed out towards S. Florida and the Keys. Tom and I laid on the cabin roof smoking our pipes, and the boat glided along, we mutually congratulated ourselves on the change from New York, with its snow and slush, its unhallowed but civilized delights, to our present enjoyment of floating along sharing that time as we went. For four days the weather blew eighteen mph, a cold North wind, the fishing was poor. The fifth day the sun shone and Tom did not wish to venture from the sailboat preferring to read and relax. I ventured forth alone up a lazy Creek, put out a silver spoon and rowed with a foot on the reel. I have always had a mania for fishing entirely alone and have found with practice calling to my aid to traits of forgotten ancestors, and using my hands and feet I could do very good trolling by myself and rode barely half a minute there was a jerk I seized the rod and brought to boat the bass that pulled my scales beyond the 12 pound notch. Casting him in the bow, I began again to fish. Minute followed the minute as I filled the boat with bass; 300 pounds of glimmering bass. Then I rowed back to the sailboat for unfortunately, a dinner of canned goods. Tom was jealous, and a sailboat I passed also had no fish, and was quite frustrated when they saw mine.

The fish he spoke of were actually channel redfish, as they are called today. As previously mentioned, catch and release was never in the minds of

anglers in the 1800s when it came to saltwater fish. There were so many fish and so few anglers that the thought of conservation was just not in the minds of so-called sportsmen of the period. In the entire article, there is no mention of eating what was caught. As with tarpon, barracuda, sailfish, marlin and bonefish, hanging them up for a picture and bragging rights was the order. This lasted all the way to more modern times. As the fish that were seen became scarcer and scarcer, writers (including myself) began turning in articles to all sport fishing magazines and newspaper columns concerning the catch, photo and release of all fish not meant for food. Also, sport fishing captains began seeing the fish as more important than to just catch once—the disappearing resource began getting a facelift in the order of respect it deserved. Several captains said that they would like their sons and perhaps their daughters to take over their sport fishing businesses, and this requires a fishy future.

Today in the Keys, almost every tournament is catch, photo and release. These events are fundraisers for important causes such as the Boy Scouts, cystic fibrosis, mental health awareness, muscular dystrophy and other disorders.

There are legendary guides, some still fishing, such as Stu Apte, Alex Adler and Scott Stanczyk, and too many who are part of the fishing days gone by, such as Jimmie Albright, Jack Brothers and Captain Bill Smith, who reportedly caught the first bonefish ever taken on "regulation fly tackle" in 1939. There are many more, far too numerous to mention. Many of these are listed in a chapter in this book. These guides were favorites of the rich and famous and anyone who can plunk down some dollars (usually about fifteen dollars per charter day). One such truly amazing individual was Captain Bob Lewis, captain of the sport fishing boat that belonged to Bob Knight, of *Knight Ridder*, *Miami Herald* and worldwide newspaper fame. Captain Lewis is also credited with bringing the fishing kite to the fishing community. Captain Lewis began manufacturing kites and kite reels in the 1950s throughout the Keys. Just about every charter boat began using them.

Opposite: In the 1800s, this was an image of a "dandy" angler with his tarpon in the Florida Keys. *Author's collection.*

Captain Bob Lewis on the *Chief* found these big eye tuna, a rarity in Keys waters. Most tuna in the Florida Keys are black fin. Captain Bob Lewis ran this boat for Bob Knight, co-owner of the *Miami Herald*. *Courtesy of IGFA.*

As Florida Keys fishing editor for the *Miami Herald*, I kept up with Ted Williams and George Bush in their Keys angling exploits. These were people who could go anywhere in the world to fish but chose to spend most of their time in the Keys, as did writer Zane Grey and Presidents Truman, Kennedy, Roosevelt, Eisenhower, Hoover and others down through history, to name a few. Ted Williams told me that his very favorite saltwater fish to tangle with was the "Silver King"—the tarpon. This is nothing new, as the tarpon had been the quarry in the 1800s that brought French counts, business magnates and erstwhile anglers from all over the world to attempt to catch this powerful fish on rod and reel. As I wrote articles for international magazines, they have brought individuals such as Mr. Lamborghini from Florence, Italy, to come fish in the Keys and many others who wanted to try their luck at tarpon, bonefish and permit. None went home without having first made, as my dear mentor Homer Circle put it, "keeper memories."

In the past, reels were bereft of great modern geared drags; friction-burned thumbs from the leather pad drag were talked about around the sportsmen's dinner tables, often sounding like they deserved the Purple Heart for their wounded digits. More often than not, lines parted company with the bony-mouthed, extremely powerful fish due to breaking lines, lines sliced by barnacles and pulled hooks due mainly to the fact that this big fish was just too fast and too strong to be held and brought to the boat or shore by anglers who were unable to control their reels and line fast enough, and deftly enough, to assist in subduing the great Silver King of inshore waters.

The main reason this fish was easily fished in days of old was accessibility. They school in relatively shallow waters and are and were accessible in great numbers. Anglers did not need to go well offshore for the truly big girls and boys—the sailfish, marlin, wahoo and swordfish—in boats that just didn't lend themselves to big-water trolling. So if there was one fish that sparked the imagination of anglers eager to fish the Florida Keys, it was the tarpon. Any angler before modern times and since who tangled with a 100-pounder-and-up-sized fish was often heard saying, "I don't know if I can hang on any more. Maybe you should take the rod." I know this is true; I uttered those words myself when I was attached to a 170-pound tarpon that just wouldn't let go after three hours one night off the Channel 5 Bridge, near Islamorada. Yes, I got her to the boat fifteen times, but lady luck was on my side as she finally swam off after the hook pulled at the boat. You might ask why I referred to this big fish as "her"? I'll leave that to your imagination.

This book is more about the history of fishing and not so much about those individual, stalwart people, who braved the early Keys without the services that are so common today—like mosquito "bug juice" spray planes, safe modern roads, electricity, restaurants, air conditioning, luxury hotels, pensions and rental rooms. However, without considering a few of them who shall stand to represent most of the others not mentioned, we can fit this book into a manageable read, not the thousands of pages it would need to be the most comprehensive possible, with all people, places and things included.

Once the roads were in, fueling stations began popping up after the railroad was blown away by the 1935 hurricane, and tracks and bridges began being paved over to make them available for commerce and the visiting angler. The road opened in 1938, but before and after the railroad, the Havana Special came to the Keys and sailing boats and ferries still made their way from Miami, bringing in bow-tied anglers from the north to fish for the Silver

King, snapper, grouper and a diminutive fish of great distinction, although small in size: the grunt. The grunt was and is a fish easily caught, and true to its moniker, it grunts profusely as it comes over the rail. These fish, together with grits that need no refrigeration, make a fine healthy, tasty meal. Grits and fresh Spanish grunts that swarmed the reefs and inside shallower waters became a staple meal for those early locals who spent their time and their lives in the Keys.

Those who knew the Keys intimately by living there were a hardy lot; they were not held back by blackened oilcloths swarmed black with mosquitoes. Modern screening in windows and bug repellants were soon introduced, and today's low-flying mosquito control airplanes, loaded with poisons, regularly began covering the Florida Keys, killing billions of mosquitoes but also impacting the mangrove-lined waters filled with fish and shrimp and an entire array of organisms that supplied a niche in the food chain, from birds to fish, crustaceans and mollusks. In the pages of this book, you will read about the way it used to be and the way it is today when fishing in the Florida Keys.

Chapter 1

Most Common Game Fish
of the Florida Keys

There are literally thousands of species of fish that swim the seas, oceans and coastal rivers of the world. The deep and shallow waters of the Florida Keys in and around Monroe County to the Gulf Stream and the Gulf of Mexico are home to many of these fish species. The Florida Keys snake thirty-five bony-island bodies (old reefs and new) out to sea. This bridge-connected island chain presents the fish that pelagically (migratorily) visit and also the fish that are year-round residents of the channels, reefs, flats and FADs (fish aggregating devices), such as recent sunken ships, the hundreds of early wrecks and other debris that form homes and cover for reef fish. In turn, these structures attract predators that feed on the fish.

For the sake of keeping it special to the Keys Gulf Stream and the Gulf of Mexico, we will feature the most common fish that have been sought by anglers and commercial fishermen in the known history of the Keys. From offshore to the reefs, to close in toward the flats and channels between the islands, there are so many species that an angler would have to live in the Keys and fish every day and night for a lifetime, and he still would not be able to catch every one of these six hundred species. These unique fish live, breed, migrate and make their home at the reef or visit the tidal channels between the Keys from Key Largo to Key West. These are just the known places, never mind the other 1,700 or more "wild" islands that make up the balance of the number of mangrove-lined islands in the sun. First seen and fished for as a game fish in the Keys was the tarpon.

Richard Stanczyk, owner of Bud N' Mary's Fishing Marina, stands next to a tarpon that the author fought as a shark came out of the blue and took a bite. Any fish that's hooked up is at a disadvantage, and sharks take advantage of this whenever they can. The shark was over ten feet long and took just one bite. *Photo by author.*

Tarpon of yesteryear were always dead trophies. The fish were so prolific and put up such an incredible and showy battle that anglers of old felt they had to show off their trophy catches. Today, almost all fishermen take a picture and save the memory—and the fish, too, by releasing it. *Courtesy of IGFA.*

Anglers in the 1800s used broomstick-sized rods and early thumb-leather dragged reels to try and tame the Silver King, so-called due to the fact that, pound for pound, this giant has more muscle than ten grown men. These big fish are evolutionarily developed and designed to propel their great bony, beautifully silver scale–adorned bodies through the strongest tides and away from the jaws of other fishes that want to make a meal of them. From the inshore sharks such as the bull and sand tiger to the offshore tiger, hammerhead and white tip, tarpon, once hooked, are at a disadvantage in fleeing these big-toothed predators. The tarpon is in the herring family and from jaw to tail in many ways resembles whole pickled herring found in the barrels of food purveyors. However, tarpon is the king of these fishes. One big reason tarpon is still around today is that it does not have a saleable value as food fish.

In the 1800s, there were no protected species laws or any other fisheries laws. This being the case, every animal and fish was fair game for anyone and everyone. So there was a large trade in turtle hunting and fishing. Big turtles such as the giant Tortugas (loggerheads) and several other species were tipped over as they made their way on and off the beaches to lay their eggs. The turtles were taken and sold for meat and shell down in Key West. Turtles were speared, dragged and butchered where they lay. Most often, as there was no reliable refrigeration, they were kept alive in kraals (water-fenced corrals). Although there are still turtles today, such as huge leatherbacks, hawks bill, smaller green and giant loggerhead turtles, they are certainly not around in the incredible numbers they once were in the Keys. Shortsightedly, their eggs were prized as much or more than chicken eggs. Today, sea turtles are federally protected, and their flesh and shells may not be taken for any use whatsoever in continental waters of the United States, or in almost all nations' waters that turtles frequent.

The following account by a visitor to the Keys in 1871, quoted from *Harper's New Monthly* magazine, 1871 edition, shows the vast difference of how these large sea turtles were talked about and considered. This was a time when the Keys was a place of plenty, with more animals and fish then there were people, and the wildness of the Keys was truly a jungle:

> *Purposing to aid the Cuban Telegraph Company, our government considered it advisable to make a reconnaissance of the great range of Keys upon the Florida Reef. The thought was to lay wire cables across the trees of the Keys all the way to Key West. It was decided that the cable across the inlets upon poles set in the mud between the islands would be interference*

for the sponge boats. So as a writer for Harper's *I went to the Keys to take a look for this story. However, subsequently a cable from Miami to Cape Sable was laid. While visiting these wild places and hearing about the big pumas that were eating the spongers and wreckers dogs, and threatening to eat the men too, I had my experiences too. Our party were now thoroughly aroused to the fact by two scared wreckers whose faces were lighted by the glare of our fires, of a first-class hunt awaiting them, and the most feasible method would be to stalk the panther, an inglorious but safe one, as even the mosquitoes would prove to be formidable in the jungle. The panther that had struck earlier would unquestionably return as he had only moistened his teeth in the flesh of the poor dog that curled up before the fire, trembling with fright and pain from his lacerated limbs, and only a taste from the ear of the hog. Fowling pieces and rifles were thoroughly inspected, and the party arranged to take watch in the wreckers hut, placing a board across the door, behind which Pableau, our cook, was stationed as a look-out. A fearful attack from the mosquitoes rendered this style of hunting far from agreeable, notwithstanding the fire was kept burning briskly before the door, ostensibly to draw them away from the house. True to his instincts the "Painter" put in an appearance about midnight. "Golly! Folks; look at them eyes!" says Pableau and bang went his rifle, out of all proper time and against orders. The creature leaped over the bushes, and crossed in full view of the blazing fire, just in time to receive a broadside from the reserve; who presented a comical appearance, crowding the doorway, aiming over the prostrate form of Pableau, who had been kicked backward by the combined effect of a big charge and fright. The monster proved to be a full-grown puma, or American lion, nearly 5-feet in length and standing more than two feet high. The beast had huge paws. Several instances of attacks have occurred in Florida, and a recent one took place. A child was seized, and the animal was making off with it rapidly, when the father gave chase; it fought desperately with the man, but a neighbor took a shot and killed it.*

On the following day the erstwhile travelers headed by sailboat from Angelfish Creek in Key Largo to Tavernier Island (where I raised my family over a 30-year period). Tavernier Creek is another one of these open water-ways quite like a river (still is) open runs produced by the tides. Here is the favorite haunt of the young sea turtles, a good feeding ground secure from numerous enemies of the outer waters (sharks). The green turtle here were found in abundance and particularly fond of seaweeds which it prefers, on which it thrives and fattens. During the breeding season they are easily taken while crawling upon the beaches to lay their

Above: This turtle tip-over graphic was made before modern cameras, and it depicts how turtles were handled during the halcyon days of the Keys. By tipping the turtles on their backs, they were disabled from returning to the sea after they laid their eggs. The eggs were highly prized as food, too. No conservation for these marine animals in the early days of the settlers' times on the Keys has severely curtailed the vast numbers that once populated Keys waters and everywhere else in the oceans. *Courtesy of J. Wilkinson, president of the Keys Historical Trust.*

Left: This is how they handled turtles caught off the Keys in 1910. They hauled them aboard and brought most of them to the turtle kraals in Key West for turtle meat and turtle shell markets. *Courtesy of J. Wilkinson, president of the Keys Historical Trust.*

Turtles, when captured, were turned over so they could not attempt escape. They also could bite, and having them on their backs kept the hunters from having fingers or toes chopped off. The jaws of a sea turtle are strong enough to bite through the shells of mollusks and decapitate a fish. *Courtesy of J. Wilkinson, president of the Keys Historical Trust.*

eggs; but many are taken by pegging, as the turtle terms it. A prism-shaped pointed steel peg is fitted to a socket in the end of a stout pole. A line holds the peg, and serves to draw the creature toward the boat after the peg is driven into the turtles shell and then the peg is loosened from the pole. Turtle hunters also tipped them over so they couldn't reach the water and gave themselves time to drag them to the boat for transport to Key West Kraals. The green turtle is most valued as an article of food, and the Key West market is usually supplied from these back bays and creeks. Also the Hawks Bill turtles caught here in abundance having excellent shell plates, or scales, so valued in jewelry and comb manufacture.

Today, forget about seeing hawks bills in Tavernier or, for that matter, green turtles as well. They can still be seen, but it will be a rare sight.

The turtle kraals of Key West held the captured bounty that was destined for meat. The shell was made into combs, brush handles, barrettes and eyeglass frames, to name a few. Until recently, the kraals were a place for tourists to view big turtles swimming in pools as they ate fish sandwiches at the tiki bars on the same premises.

The takers of all sea turtles today are subject to a $20,000 federal fine and possible jail time. Sea turtles are on top of the endangered species list in the United States. Only the Cayman Islands now have a species of sea turtles they raise that are used in commercial situations. No turtle products, including the shell or otherwise, are legal to sell in the United States and most other countries.

The following are some of the most common offshore fish and inshore species. They played a role in attracting commercial fisherman to the Keys and then, later, sport fisherman, with their particular traits, food value and feeding habits during the past 150 years.

Amberjack

This giant member of the jack family grows to weights in excess of 100 pounds. However, today the fish are in the 15- to 80-pound range due to heavy fishing pressure supplying fast-food fry houses. The world record of 155 pounds, 12 ounces, is noted in the IGFA record book. In days of yore, these fish were captured using cut baits of barracuda, whole Spanish grunts, small snapper, mullet, ballyhoo and the king of baits: Florida crawfish. Today, amberjack are still caught with any cut, or a strip of fish, that the angler could fit on a 6/0 or larger hook. They can also be taken with a heavy jig, and baits must be dropped with a fishing sinker weight, from 6 ounces to 1 pound.

Amberjack live deep, around wrecks and reefs, in, off and around the Florida Keys and well into the Gulf of Mexico. About fifteen miles offshore of Islamorada, there is a location called the Hump—basically a hill in the Gulf Stream whose sides drop off to hundreds of feet in depth. When a heavily weighted bait is dropped close to or over the top, this often would elicit a strong, solid pull of (in the old days, before big fish houses began taking their toll by wholesale slaughter for the fish-and-chips, fish-sandwich franchises of America) a large amberjack.

Snake Creek Fishing Camp was just off the famous Snake Creek cut. Once under the bridge to the ocean, it was a straight-run amberjack. *Courtesy of historian Irving Eyster.*

The amberjack is a favorite food fish in the offshore shark food chain; it fights hard, does not surface and jump, is a very wormy fish, pulls hard and strong and really gives a workout to a deep-sea angler pulling heavy weight and jerking muscle from the depths. This, as all fish, is a beautiful fish with an amber-colored flash of color bleeding into a dark coloration near the eyes.

Charter captains in the past, when nothing else was biting closer to the surface, on the troll would take their fishing charters to hook these fish. They were usually able to get one or two fish per person, and this was enough to put sweat on the brow and strain on the muscles of even the fittest angler. I know, as my first amberjack at the Hump in my friends Al and Harry's boat was a 115-pounder in 1978. I still remember the bicep strain today. That same day, my second amberjack hauled up from the deep was taken by a ten-foot mako shark. The fast and powerful toothy shark bit the fish in half,

A prehistoric shark tooth and rhino molar found in a coastal river mud bottom by Vito Bertucci. The shark tooth would be from a Megaladon shark in the sixty-foot range. It has been said that Bertucci drowned while pursuing his life-long quest of finding shark and other animals that lived in today's American waters millions of years ago. He also may have had a heart attack while diving in muddy, swift waters that could have trapped him on an underwater obstruction. *Photo by author.*

and then, when it felt the hook, it took a fifteen-foot jump indelibly etched in my mind's eye thirty-five years later. No, we didn't catch the mako; it caught us forever!

THE GREAT ATLANTIC BARRACUDA

That barred "wolf of the sea" has been a notorious game fish down through the history of fishing in southern waters. This toothy, slicing and dicing fish is the saltwater equivalent of the muskellunge in fresh water. But barracudas are tougher. They live in the "big lakes"—the oceans and seas—with tides and currents and bigger and meaner fish like sharks to escape from. They are faster than their freshwater near look-alikes. Inshore off the flats and channels of the Keys, these fish are sought after for their strong initial runs and high-flying first leaps after they are hooked. Their dental work is such that they can slice through virtually any fish, hand or foot that gets near their mouths. Often, if someone is bitten, it's because they trail something shiny around their necks or on their wrists while swimming, diving or washing or flash a filet knife at the dock where the 'cudas are used to feeding on filleted pieces of fish that the anglers toss overboard from the cleaning table. Anything with sharp teeth such as 'cuda and sharks is sought for game as anglers from near and far want to catch these fish as trophies. However, the barracuda is a fish-eating animal, and people are not on their diet. Typically, if you're sliced and dismembered by a 'cuda, it was done by the fish on an instinctive level of striking something that it perceived as a flashing, darting fish. The great barracuda grows to over eighty pounds, with a world record of eighty-five pounds (today, fish are more in the eight- to forty-pound sizes). There are several varieties worldwide, but for the Keys, the great barracuda is the fish that anglers have caught since fishing's beginnings. A flashy baitfish, a silver spoon or a tube lure takes these fish. Cut baits or strips of mullet or ballyhoo take them too. 'Cuda are a tasty fish but if eaten can contain nerve-damaging ciguatera.

BONEFISH

If the tarpon is king of inshore fish with its high-flying, multiple jumps; bony, tough mouth; and head-shaking act, then the bonefish is speed demon of the flats. The bonefish looks like it is diamond studded. Its scales are like shining white jewels. Virtually any angler who has a chance to feel a bonefish run will never again think of fishing as a boring sport. I personally have boated and released several hundred bonefish over a thirty-year period, and I can attest to the one hundred yards of line taken off my reel spool in mere seconds. If I did not have a properly set drag and smoothing lithium grease, I probably would have lost most of those fish to snapped lines—from three-pounders up to my personal largest, seventeen-plus-pound (probably a world record on eight-pound monofilament, but it was photographed and released before IGFA had a catch and release division in their record books). Sight fishing for this silver ghost is so-called due to the difficulty of seeing this fish easily on the flats without Polarized glasses. Often even with these glasses comes the problem of "now-you-see-them, now-you-don't" experiences. It's no wonder many fish easily disappear like water-borne ghosts.

Shrimp, small crabs, artificial crab lures, shrimp-flies and small pink and white jigs take this speedster. They don't bite hard on the line, but their crusher mouths do bite the bait; once hooked, they are an awe-inspiring fishing experience. President George Herbert Walker Bush loves to fish for bonefish: "My favorite fish in Florida is the bonefish, and it truly is a fish to reckon with when I visit America's Caribbean Islands."

COBIA

Based on the fact that the Keys (except for Key West) were really not equipped to accommodate anglers before the railroad came into being—expeditions were the way so-called sport fishermen described their sailboat adventures to the Keys, towing canoes—very little offshore fishing was done. In land-based camps, for a number of reasons, not the least of which were mosquitoes, wild animals, no roads and no railroads, general living comforts were minimalist at best. So migratory fish in deep water, such as the cobia or "crab eater," were not common fish to target like those ever-present in shallower waters—tarpon, grouper and snapper groups.

Cobia look a lot like sharks, and to novices they appear to be sharks. But these fish love grunts, crabs and other mouth-sized baits. Their slightly yellowish flesh tastes quite a bit like their favorite food: crabs. A hard-fighting fish hosted by large stingrays, they swim in small groups and, once hooked, really pull hard. In the early days, cobias were large, tough customers. They were easy to hook, but good strong tackle with excellent drags were a must then, as now. The world-record cobia came in at 136 pounds. Many cobias in the 20- to 60-pound class are caught in Keys waters as they migrate south along the edge of the Gulf Stream, where they can be found in some fifteen- to forty-foot depths. Captains look for large stingrays, and then mates and anglers cast live baits toward the rays, hopeful for a confrontation with a sybaritic cobia. Spanish grunts, pinfish and mullet are all lollipops to the cobia, but their name comes from the Spanish *cabeo*, meaning "crab eater."

Atlantic Bonito

A smaller member of the tuna family, the bonito is a favorite prey for about every billfish such as marlin, sailfish and swordfish, as well as sharks, wahoo and king mackerel. The fish swim fast, and marauding schools terrorize flying fish and any fry of any fish that swims. Trolled feathers and jigs cast at a working school, smaller ballyhoo and finger mullet and strip baits from dolphin belly to mullet or 'cuda take these offshore pelagic fish. The world record is eighteen pounds, four ounces. But a ten-pounder is a big bonito. As with all offshore fish, bonito have been plentifully caught since boats became motorized and could safely run out deep and return irrespective of wind direction or speed, tides and currents, which always had to be taken into account before reliable boat motors came on the fishing scene. To me, Bonito are a fishy-tasting fish, but they are great bait for marlin and make excellent strip baits for trolling.

Dolphin

Today, the dolphin fish (mahi-mahi in Hawaii) is one of the most sought-after game fish off Keys shores. It's no wonder, as they are easy to catch when found around flotsam and jetsam, weed lines or anything offering shade to their bait prey, and their white-fleshed meat tastes very good. These fish run in schools and are the most colorful game fish that can be found in Keys waters. Often, they can be caught near the reef that runs down the full length of the Florida Keys on the deep side, just off the Gulf Stream. In years past (early 1900s), these fish were trolled for by the sailing skiffs as they ran from the mainland toward Key West and across to Cuba. Dolphin school from down south toward the Keys. When the waters warm, they move past the Keys and run north all the way up and past the Carolinas. They are pelagic and are most frequently caught during late spring and summer months in Keys waters. Anglers today, as yesterday, look for anything floating in the distance, especially if there are birds circling that area. Dolphins are caught in sizes ranging from five to thirty-five pounds. However, often bull and cow dolphins in the forty- to fifty-pound range can also be hooked up. The world all-tackle record is just over eighty-eight pounds. Yellow, blue and gold, these acrobatic fish begin fading on deck or in the fish box; they turn to a silvery gray. White-fleshed and tasty, dolphin is fried, broiled and baked for a fabulous meal.

According to sporting magazines in the early twentieth century, the fish most talked about was the most inedible of all the game fish that swim in Keys waters: the tarpon. The reason why dolphin was not a fish targeted in those days was because it is an offshore fish. Without reliable motors and truly seagoing vessels available for offshore fishing, the majority of sport fishing was done inshore. Dolphins feed on flying fish, small sea turtles, crabs and every little fish that takes shelter under a Sargasso weed forest and other floating weeds and debris. Once a dolphin is hooked, other fish in the school competitively hang around, so many are caught for the box because of this. The dolphin fish is a very important fish for all offshore charter boats today. Once found, they are easy to catch, and they make the day for their charter customers with their colorful jumping antics and their excellent food value.

The Grouper and Snapper Clan

From the giant jewfish (today called goliath grouper), the Nassau grouper, gag grouper, black grouper, red hinds grouper, yellow grouper, snowy grouper, rainbow grouper and more make up the species. The jewfish or goliath hangs around bridge pilings, in and around wrecks and near large cave-like reef structures. These giant fish suck in their prey. The mouth on a six-hundred-pound goliath is large enough to capture and feed on almost any size fish, including small sharks in the nurse shark group. A size 10/0 and up (shark hooks work well) and, in the past, a nice lobster are great bait. However, almost anything like a big chunk of 'cuda, a head of a cut-up amberjack or a live jack or porgy works great too.

Because of having been overfished, all goliath grouper are now released. These fish in and around Keys bridges were caught and delivered to Miami fish houses to be used for ground-up chum. Grouper grow large compared to other reef fishes such as snapper. Typically, grouper range from 3 to 85 pounds, with the aforementioned bucket-mouth goliath reaching up to 600 pounds (the world record is 680 pounds, caught in Florida in 1961). All grouper inhale virtually anything they can get into their large, bucket-sized mouths.

In the past, Florida lobster was a preferred bait, not only for grouper, but for all large predator fish, including the cubera snapper, which grows to 100 pounds or more (the IGFA record is a 124-pounder), the largest of the thirty-eight different kinds of snappers that swim the reefs of the Florida Keys.

Except for the cubera, you won't see a fisherman use a lobster for bait; they'll eat it themselves. Live mullet, pinfish and grunts both white and Spanish, as well as cut baits of barracuda or dolphin pieces that are deep dropped with weights that can reach down and through the currents will take any of the grouper clan. But something that no one but a reef fisherman would know is that grouper have a secret weapon. Almost every grouper, once hooked, races toward the reef hidey-hole, or rock pile, swims in headfirst and flares its gills. They basically lock themselves in so the fisherman cannot pull them out; believe me, it works, and the only way to possibly catch that fish is by immediately releasing the pressure. Once it feels safe,

President George Herbert Walker Bush loves to fish, and the Keys is a favorite place. He loves bonefishing and permit fishing. During an Everglades Conservation fundraiser, we discussed the state of the Union (that is, the fishy state of the Union). *Photo by author.*

it usually will swim out of the hole. If the fisherman has grunt power, he or she can really put the pressure on and get the fish away from the bottom protective cover and pump it skyward to the net, gaff or over the gunnels for the smaller ones.

A favorite fish in the Keys and throughout Florida is the mangrove snapper. Probably the most caught fish in the Keys, these fish are very wary, especially when they get over ten inches in length. These smart fish have sharp, strong teeth (called snappers as they snap their jaws closed, and you best have your digits out of the way), and they love shrimp. They are mostly caught off Keys bridges and around any of the piers and islands channels and undercut banks of the Keys. Another popular snapper is called the mutton snapper, so called as it is shaped like a leg of mutton. This reef snapper grows big and strong. Found around rocks, reefs and any sunken ships, it is a prized food fish. These larger members of the snapper family love small grunts and any live and cut baits. Stout tackle is needed for these bruisers. When fish traps were introduced over the reefs (now outlawed), they would catch these fish, as well as other snapper and grouper.

Today, one of the most popular fish to catch and eat in the Keys is the yellowtail snapper. A delicate and tasty fish, it fights hard, and its run, once hooked, is likened to the first run of a bonefish. Although a far smaller fish than a bonefish, a three-pound yellowtail can snap a ten-pound test line if the reel's drag isn't set just right. These are schooling fish and require chum to bring them up from the depths off the reefs. President George H. Bush told me it's his favorite fish to eat. The Cheeca Lodge, in the 1990s, served the "Presidential Snapper," so named in honor of President George H. Bush, who frequently fished and ate this snapper dish at the lodge. He always made sure to ask for a salad instead of broccoli.

BLACK FIN TUNA

The black fin tuna is a schooling fish. All of the tuna clan swim in schools. Pound for pound, it is a very hard-fighting member of the clan. Black on its back and shaped like a large football with a tail, it makes excellent eating and is caught usually in the five- to thirty-five-pound range. A world record forty-nine-pound fish was caught off Marathon, in the Florida Keys. Tuna love anything alive that they can chase for a meal. They strike feathers, spoons, strip baits and just about anything that flashes. However, when in a feeding frenzy, they will take cut pieces of bait as well. Today, some fly-fishing anglers ask their charter captains for the opportunity to catch them on a saltwater fly. Up until relatively recent times, offshore fly-fishing was just not done. Black fin tuna are caught well offshore. They were not a species that early Keys anglers targeted, nor was there this new furor over catching big fish on what was considered freshwater lighter tackle. Now, manufacturers offer great modern gear made of new space-age materials that can actually handle big powerful fish such as tuna, small marlin, sailfish, wahoo and other speedy tough-on-gear critters. After the turn of the twentieth century, with the advent of more modern boat motors attached to highly

Boatwright Fishing Camp. The sign says, "Boatwright Fishing Camp—charter boat—two motors—deep sea bay fishing—row boats $1.00 day." Early fish camps made it very easy for visitors to come and get their bait, boat and gear at prices that were commensurate with those times and places: cheaply! *Courtesy of J. Wilkinson, president of the Keys Historical Trust.*

seaworthy boats, tuna, like a host of other offshore game fish, were found at the docks for fileting. They were caught with gear more related to light winches attached to broomstick-thick rods.

Cero Mackerel

Smaller than king mackerel and with a telltale yellow line along their flanks, these excellent-tasting and hard-fighting fish were targeted as commercial fish during their migrations. They do get over the reef and into relatively shallower waters, and they were reachable by even the paddled skiffs of old. Lighter tackle with jigs and silver spoons, cut baits, small baitfish like finger-sized mullet and little thread herring dropped back and cast on smaller conventional bass-type, bait-casting reels were used before the spinning reel came on the sport fishing scene. There was no monofilament before

This image is of the IGFA research section of its E.K. Harry Library, located upstairs at the IGFA Fishing Hall of Fame & Museum in Dania, Florida. This section of the library is a repository of gear and information on sport fishing's early halcyon days. *Photo by author.*

the 1940s, only linen and dacron lines. Earlier lines were of horsehair, then linen with catgut and even silk leaders. Lines of old had to be dried after each use. Compared to modern lines of monofilament and special fibers, they were not long lasting and abrasion resistant, either. The cero mackerel grow to seventeen pounds, and the world record is a seventeen-pound, two-ounce fish caught in Florida Keys Islamorada waters in 1986. These fish are so prized for food that chances are great that larger ones in past decades were caught before there were records kept by IGFA. This goes for all fish described in this book.

KINGFISH: THE KING OF MACKEREL

This mackerel has been a staple in both the commercial fisheries and, later, in tournament fishing in the Keys. However, today it is still targeted off Texas, Alabama and the Gulf Coast. Most Keys tournaments target catch and release of basically non-food fish such as tarpon and sailfish. However, there are still dolphin fish tournaments in the Key Largo area. King mackerel, having been decimated off Keys waters by commercial overfishing and the fact that it is truly a pelagic fish, spends less time in Keys waters, so timing tournaments for it has been difficult at best. Tournaments in the Keys circuits, except for the big Key West Kingfish Tournament, target more easily available resident fish such as bonefish, redfish, summer dolphin and winter sailfish.

The kingfish, once reaching sizes over ninety pounds with a world record of more than ninety-three pounds caught in Puerto Rican waters, is caught off the Keys today in weights from twenty-five to seventy pounds. A friend, Richard Jacobs, whose father fished in Bimini, showed me pictures of kingfish that were over one hundred pounds, but of course they were caught well before the IGFA began and records were taken. Today, there is no question that with huge catch pressure on these and other great fish, they would be getting smaller and smaller.

The kingfish, as far as size, is second in weight only to its cousin the wahoo. Stripe-sided, beauteous wahoo can reach up to 150 pounds. Kings appear to be cat-like when attacking any live bait they can put their scissor-toothed mouths on. I saw 40-pounders and larger soar out of the water some fifteen feet high, chasing tethered live bait such as mullet, live trolled ballyhoo or little tuna, and their demeanor and faces actually appeared animated like a cat after a mouse. They literally pounce, slice and dice their quarry. Wire leaders are a must for these fish. In the past, piano wire was twisted onto relatively large 5/0 to 8/0 hooks. The little tuna (smallest of the tuna species), called "tunny," runs in huge schools and is a favorite bait for marlin, too. However, with lighter tackle than a broomstick, they fight hard and are a beautifully streamlined, torpedo-of-a-fish that take feathered troll baits, flashy spoons, strip baits from the belly of a dolphin fish, mullet strip, ballyhoo or other smaller baits. A great experience is to see a school chasing little flying fish. Just about any big offshore billfish, including sharks, love these little football-shaped fish, often seen in schools measuring an acre or more.

PERMIT

The permit is the largest member of the pompano clan. Elusive today compared to when they knew little of man and would quickly and easily take a crab bait, the permit is a beautiful, silver-dollar, roundish fish that loves crabs, shrimp and other mollusks. Its sickle-shaped tail was often seen in and around the mud flats, fanning the air above a mudding it made as it searched for crabs, but permit also swim offshore and hang around buoys and wrecks. The world record for a permit is sixty pounds, and it was caught in Brazilian waters in 2002. However, many thirty-five- to forty-five-pounders have been caught in the Keys. The average-size permits now caught are from about eight to forty pounds. In the past, if an angler could hold on to them, fifty- to sixty- or even seventy-pounders were around in reasonable numbers (before record keeping at the IGFA). A seventy-five-pounder was speared by Harry Snow, the man who supplied fish for the road workers. Snow probably turned out to be the first fishing guide who lived in the Keys, according to Mark Sosin, IGFA inductee to its Hall of Fame. The fish pulled loose of the spear, and for years afterward, that fish was seen by many fishermen. The scar of that spear wound was quite visible, according to Mark Sosin. To his knowledge, no one ever got close enough to cast to that fish either.

Several years ago, I caught a thirty-five-pounder in Key West waters. It was one of the very best light-tackle battles of my fishing career. I witnessed something that day that I'll never forget. As I fought one of a pair of permit, which mate for life, its mate repeatedly struck my fishing line as if to break his mate off. My wife, Barb, and the guide witnessed this. Once we had the fish to boat for photo and release, the permit's mate stayed close to the boat, and they both swam hurriedly away once its mate was free. It was just one of many experiences I have had showing fishes' fidelity to their mates.

The true sportsman's trifecta of a catch in the Keys is catching a tarpon, bonefish and permit all in one day. It appears that from the early days of sports fishing clubs (including the 1920s Long Key Club, which was visited by President Hoover and other famous Americans), this special sports designation was sought after by all members and their guests. Few accomplished this. The reason was that in those times, each fish of the trifecta required different techniques and gear to be able to make this happen. Some diehards spent their time at the club trying for many years and failed to have "trifecta lightning" strike them.

POMPANO

There are eight different pompano species in the *IGFA World Record Game Fishes* book, but the one most popular and often caught is the Florida pompano. The all-tackle world record for this fish is just over eight pounds. They were so common and easy to catch during the heyday of South Florida being opened up by Flagler's railroad that they were served as the haute cuisine at every hotel restaurant up and down the East Coast. The pompano is an incredibly tasty fish. It takes jigs and various small lures, but it loves little sand crabs. These fish, like all other fish, are a product of what they consume as far as taste and even texture of flesh. From 1900 until today, they have been very sought after for game and table.

David Epstein, the author's oldest son, with a pompano he caught on a busman's holiday from the U.S. Air Force. *Photo by author.*

REDFISH

Redfish are actually red drum fish. These fish are targeted as game fish in the Keys and along the West Coast as one of the most fun fish to catch on a jig or gold spoon (excluding the showy snook, tarpon and racy bonefish). The world record, according to the IGFA, is over ninety-four pounds. They are fun fish to target, and many Keys sportsmen head over toward the Everglades area of Shark River to fish for them. They take shrimp, crab, small minnows and about anything that moves or looks like it could be tasty. In the past, coastal rivers were awash with them. The larger they get, the grainier their flesh is for the table. These fish fight hard and bulldog all the way to the boat.

SNOOK

The snook is found around backwater, undercut mangrove islands, shore, bridges and piers. These black, lateral-lined fish are ambush fish. They grow large, and the most often caught kind is the common snook in the Keys (there are about eight different varieties of snook). They hit hard, they jump and they are spectacular game fish. They are also the very best tasting inshore fish in southern, saltwater environs. The all-tackle record, according to the IGFA, is fifty-three pounds. I caught a twenty-nine-pounder once, and it made for a lifetime memory on light tackle. They love finger mullet and shrimp, as well as anything live that they can ambush and inhale. Great lures are jigs with deer hair, such as Millie's buck tails and soft bait, as well as DOA lures in shrimp colors. In the early days of Miami, snook were called "soap fish" and discarded dead as trash fish. Oh, if they only knew what they were missing out on! No one throws them away now. They are so prized that most are released after a quick kiss by a happy angler.

SAILFISH

This showy fish with the large dorsal fin is the "dandy" of the waves. The fish displays the largest dorsal fin of any fish, anywhere at any time. This billfish is truly the darling of sport fishermen worldwide. It's not the largest of the billfish; actually, with the exception of the spearfish, which is almost

"Dandies" with their sailfish in the 1920s. The fish were caught in the Gulf Stream off Key Largo. *Photo courtesy of the IGFA.*

always smaller, it is diminutive in comparison to blue, striped, white, black marlin and, of course, the swordfish.

In the early days of the twentieth century, there probably wasn't a lawyer's office or a banker's office wall that did not have a skin-mounted sailfish arching its back behind their desks. Even a small sailfish makes a magnificent picture with its gorgeous sail and sickle tail and slim-lined head and bill.

In the early 1900s until perhaps the 1930s, sailfish were called the "boo-hoo fish." This referred to how they jumped baits that were meant for king mackerel. Anglers were supposedly so upset that their "shot" at a king mackerel was spoiled by the non-edible sailfish (they are great smoked) that some even cried about it. Nevertheless, the sailfish in the Keys is a pelagic beauty and loves to strike ballyhoo, flying fish, trolled fish strips or mullet, or when they are easily cast to, a fat live pilchard will also do the trick. These fish are acrobatic and are about the fastest fish in the ocean, with the exception of the wahoo.

Captain Nick Stanczyk with a huge daytime-caught swordfish, caught with his uncle Captain Scott Stanczyk, his father, Richard, and friends on the *Catch 22* charter boat berthed at Bud N' Mary's Fishing Marina. The Stanczyks have repioneered daytime swordfishing, after many years of trial and error out in the Gulf Stream trying to locate and bait them for hookups. They succeeded so well that the marina has become "swordfish central" for those wanting to duel with these fish with swords. *Courtesy of Captain Nick Stanczyk.*

Using medium gear and fought while standing up, not hoisting these mostly thirty-five- to seventy-five-pound fish when sitting down in a fighting chair with big sticks and reels, they are a fabulous game fish whose fight and spunkiness will treat the angler to a lifetime of memories.

Although slim and sleek, Atlantic sailfish (Pacific are bigger fish) are a long fish, in six- to nearly nine-foot lengths. Sailfish, like all the billfish clan, should be released after a photo. But in days of yore, as the tarpon's fate was sealed once captured, the sailfish, too, felt the bite of the gaff. The fish were summarily hung up for photo and bragging rights. However, smoked, the sailfish actually is quite good, but this was not usually done; rather, the fish were usually wasted. This is rarely the case for the mightiest of the billfish caught offshore of the Keys. The meat of a swordfish is highly prized (yet poisonous mercury is found in its flesh now; doctors recommend that pregnant women don't eat it) as a food fish that could ultimately cause its final undoing if this big billfish is not properly managed.

Sailfish Strategies

That large, highly deployed dorsal fin from which the sailfish received its moniker is not just a swimming fin; it's also used to fool and herd baitfish. The sailfish deploys this fin as sort of a barrier to its prey as it swoops in for the kill. A pod of sailfish will encircle a school of baitfish and frighten them into a ball of writhing, darting fish, and then, one by one, the sails will strike at them and feed. Charter captains talk of and get mighty excited about the "showering baits," when in shallower waters sailfish rush in and cause the schooling baits to flee skyward to escape the maws of the sails. Kingfish and other predators also "shower baits," but the really big bait runs close to the reef are often, during sailfish season, the work of the billfish attempting to "ball" (herd) the baits. They make headlong rushes at the schools of ballyhoo, pilchards or flying fish, to name but a few of the schooling fish sailfish target. Showering baits sparkle and flash when struck by sunlight. The scene jump-starts the hearts of everyone aboard with its beauty and the anticipation of the action that can follow this phenomenon.

What is so exciting to anglers is the expectation and the fact that sails readily take a live bait cast at them when they are in a feeding mood. These are large fish, and their spectacular runs and airborne tactics thrill any angler who is not brain-dead. In the past, sailfish were killed, and many were smoked and many more made into mounts. But today, you can get the best mount possible by just calling in the dimensions of your fish after you photo and release it. The mount for this or any other fish done by the mount mold method (which you'll get no matter what, unless you specify for a more expensive skin mount) will not shrink, shrivel or develop fat-drip stains and will not eventually give a malodorous smell to your workplace or den during humid periods.

SEA TROUT

The sea trout is in the drum family of fishes. It looks much like a freshwater trout but is a very different breed of fish. This is a schooling fish during its juvenile life. It grows to become a top predator. Sea trout strike out on their own, or at least not in schools, when very large. In northern regions of the East Coast, these fish are called weakfish. The reason for this name is that they have very weak mouths that a hook tears, and this allows the fish to lose the hook easily. A fun and tasty fish, they hit jigs, top water lures and natural baits such as shrimp and small fish. Usually they are caught over relatively shallow sea grass flats. They are traditional fish that were taken and eaten by the Calusa Indians, later the Spanish and English and then by settlers. They are wormy in summer, but most of the year, although quite soft fleshed, they are a tried and true fish for the plate. They hone in on any disturbance on the surface by anglers' baits that gurgle and pop. This popping sound mimics the way fish feed on surface-fleeing baitfish. Early fish houses targeted them for sale. Along with Spanish and king mackerel, untold and tallied barrels of sea trout were sent north on Flagler's railroad for the restaurant and fish house trade. Sea trout grow large, and sixteen-pounders used to be common, but being overfished, they, too, are now much smaller in size.

There are so many fish that can be added to this chapter, but it would take a book the size of an encyclopedia to mention them all.

Chapter 2

Indigenous People and Indian Key

There is an eleven-acre island between Upper and Lower Matecumbe called Indian Key. Archaeologists have determined that it was inhabited by Indians over two thousand years ago and up to the 1500s. In 1513, according to Irving Eyster (a preeminent Keys historian since the 1940s and a writer), the island became a Spanish trading post and later, on February 4, 1836, the first seat of Dade County. Most of the history of this Keys island is documented between 1820 and August 7, 1840. At about that time, the village was set upon; several people were killed, and the village was burned by the Indians. Various reasons in recent history were offered as to why this occurred. The one I believe is that there was a bounty of twenty dollars for the scalps of Indians on the mainland. This was placed on the heads of the Seminoles by Dr. Perrine (one of these island's prominent residents). When the Seminole chief heard about it, he decided to fix those responsible for this bounty. That was the end of habitation on Indian Key.

Forty years ago, when I visited Indian Key, I was able to see the foundations of some of the early homes and find charred wood pieces as well. The Calusa (spelled Caloosa today) were an Indian tribe whose members were often in communities numbering up to four thousand people. The Tequesta Indians also lived in the Keys. However, the Calusa are most often described as having met up with Ponce De León. Both tribes and sub-tribes fished and gathered shellfish and crustaceans in Keys waters. The Indians also fished at night by the light of torches with spears, nets and traps. Fish were mainly smoked (salt was available from saltwater evaporation, but no actual evidence exists that

The Miccosukee Indian bride of Chief Tiger of the Musa Isle Miccosukee tribe.
Courtesy of IGFA.

These Indian artifacts of stone and bone, collected over a thirty-year period, were used by the Indians of the Keys and the South before the white man's arrival from Spain and Europe. *Courtesy of the author, private collection.*

this was done). Fish and seafood were used in stews and roasted over coals and flames or eaten raw. After 1500s, seafood was used in a ceviche's mode, pickled in citrus oil and also dried in the tropical sun. Besides fish being speared and netted, hand lines, hand-carved stone sinkers and gorges made of bone and wood were used. The Indians also fashioned hooks out of bone, shells, wood, collected mollusks and other marine animals by hand.

There were large amounts of the huge mammalian manatees (sea cow, as they are also called) speared. Later, when settlers lived in the Keys, manatees were even herded into an open-ended cut. Today called the "Cow Pens," it is a major natural gulf-side boating cut just off Tavernier Key, through the Intracoastal Waterway. This waterway was deep enough for a sailboat keel's draft.

The Calusa were killed off by disease. When the Spaniards arrived, the Indians had no built-up immunities for their foreign diseases, and they died off from them. Later on, lands once inhabited by these early peoples were taken over by the wreckers. Indian Key took on a whole new persona, and the real money on this little island was from the wreckers. Indian Key became a

The manatee grows to nearly a ton in weight and is strictly vegetarian. Docile to a fault, it is a major player in the history of the Florida Keys. These large water mammals often have propeller blade cuts that seem to heal well with big scars, but many are cut down by boats and motors. Today, in much of Keys and Florida waters, there is a special go-slow zone wherever there may be manatees basking on the surface or seen in and around canals and waterways. *Photo by author.*

wrecker's village. Wreckers risked their lives to save the people on distressed ships, despite their reputation, which was unsavory at best and bordered on piracy. However, there were no lights on the reefs and no Coast Guard to call. Maps of those times were more artful than accurate for navigation purposes. These wreckers (mostly tough, honest and hardworking men) worked in storms and hurricanes. For their efforts, they received a portion or percentage of what the actual salvage was worth.

Prior to the wreckers on Indian Key, first the Indians lived there for generations and then fishermen, explorers and even pirates were using Indian Key, a few as a base and some as they needed to on their way to or from various pursuits. These people needed and used the only freshwater wells in the entire area that were on nearby Lower Matecumbe. It was much later on that this little island became a wrecker's home and business base. Around 1820, a store was built for Captain Appleby and a Mr. Snyder. A boom in business began on the island. A boardinghouse opened to cater to the many passengers on ships anchoring in the harbor next to the island. Today, there is only a small, sturdy pier that can accommodate small boats for visitors. This historically interesting island now has no inhabitants, with perhaps only the ghosts of those killed by Indians, accidents at the wrecks and during hurricanes. During the 1820s, ship's carpenters and even a blacksmith shop opened at the end of the long-gone wharf.

Also in the 1820s, sea captain John Jacob Houseman, whose family was in the shipping business in New Jersey, moved to Indian Key to become a wrecker. He decided that he could do better if he didn't head to Key West. In Key West, he would have to deal with the judges, who decided what percentages of the wrecks were to be paid to the wreckers. However, the Key West wreckers almost always received less than those at Indian Key and Key Vaca. So Houseman chose Indian Key, which he figured was also out in the Atlantic and closer to the reefs than anywhere else in the Keys. He had the advantage of being first to the wreck and having the title of master wrecker. With this title, he could call the shots on who received what for their efforts. In July 1831, Houseman bought the store and several real estate lots. Houseman then built his home to accommodate himself and his bride, Elizabeth. He built a warehouse, wharves and houses for his workers and cisterns for rainwater.

In May 1834, Dr. Waterhouse became the first postmaster on Indian Key. A hotel called the Tropical Hotel, with a ballroom and bowling alley, was built. It was advertised as a health resort. Waterhouse and his son died in a storm as they crossed over to Lower Matecumbe. Then a Mr. Howe, a Mason, held the first Masonic Lodge meeting in Florida on Indian Key.

A lot of history for an eleven-acre island, but it continued on until after Dr. Perrine came to the island on Christmas Day 1838. Howe and Perrine incorporated the Tropical Plant Company with a nursery farm on Lower Matecumbe. They were growing plants to start a new industry in the United States. There were several settlements in the Keys that had been attacked by Indians; many of those people came to Indian Key for safety, nearly doubling the population. Nearby, at Tea Table Key, a navy base was established known as Fort Paulding. But this protection did not help when the Indians attacked Indian Key and left it burning and in smoldering ruins on August 7, 1840. At two o'clock in the morning, the Indians came and looted and then burned all but two buildings on the island belonging to Mr. Howe. In an 1871 article, it was explained that "Howe was nice and accommodating to the Indians, so they spared him and his property." However, they killed off and burned everything else, partly fueled by the rum they consumed when they raided the store. Six people were known dead. Dr. Perrine was shot and burned in his house. A Captain John Mott, his wife and their children, a four-year-old and a four-month-old, were killed in their hiding place. A thirteen-year-old, James Sturdy, died while he hid in the warehouse cistern. Others escaped by hiding and heading out into the water from their turtle kraal. After the village was destroyed, the navy moved over to Indian Key. The history of Indian Key as far as settlers were concerned was over, but the little island still exudes great history.

Indian Key was used to assemble the big Alligator Lighthouse that had to be put together in sections and installed on the reef. The lighthouse quickly became a popular place for all manner of fish such as snapper, jewfish (today called goliath grouper), sheepshead, grunts, barracuda, pompano, permit and snook, to name just a few of these fine game fish. All manner of small fish congregated for the shelter the lighthouse offered. This was the reason predators also visited the area around the lighthouse. Today, charter boats and private boats troll past the lighthouse for barracuda when all else fails. When it's too rough for comfort for the fisherman in the offshore seas and other fish are not biting, the barracuda can usually be counted on. 'Cuda give a great showing when the hook finds its mark in their jaws. This toothy fish makes a very swift run and takes at least one terrific jump. The fish then makes several powerful runs before finally coming to the boat. Novice anglers feel they really have accomplished a fine sporting move by catching one of these gamey fish. Their teeth add to the thrill of the moment, but they really are quite easy to hook and catch with the right gear and a drag properly adjusted so they don't break off on their initial run. The lighthouse is also a sea bird's best friend. Cormorants, pelicans and other sea birds perch and rest, then dive after the teeming baitfish that have sought shelter around the legs and base of the lighthouse.

Back in history, Indian Key remained the Dade County seat until it was moved to Fort Dallas (Miami) on March 4, 1844. In 1866, the Keys once again became part of Monroe County. The very first permanent settlers were called "Conchs." They were called this if they were of British descent. They came by way of the Bahamas and were dependent on the sea for their livings. These settlers were probably Eleutheran adventurers or Loyalists to the British Crown. After the Revolutionary War, they moved to the Bahamas. These people were mostly wealthy conservatives and were given property by King George III. Several generations later, their descendants came to the Keys after they had properly stripped and used up their heritage of natural resources in the Bahamas, and they left many of their slaves there. Those slaves' ancestors are now the main inhabitants of the Bahamas. The Eleutheran adventurers left England in 1647. They were looking for religious freedom but were wrecked in Nassau on New Providence Island. It took them quite a while, but they repaired their ships and headed for Eleuthera, where they settled. *Eleuthera* means "free" in German, and some of their descendants remain there to this day. Others came to Florida and the Keys.

In 1862, Congress passed the Homestead Act. The deal was that any citizen who would live on public land for five years and improve it would be able to acquire 160 acres free of charge. The island of Upper Matecumbe was acquired for under twenty dollars, which covered only the filing fees. Three families from the Bahamas basically were given this property. In that time period, Upper Matecumbe was a jungle and took a huge amount of work to clear by hand. They dealt with unforgiving amounts of mosquitoes, hurricanes and storms. Whatever they didn't pay for this island, they earned in extremely hard work and conditions. Animals for any farming in those days were fair prey for mosquitoes, so most of the protein consumed was fish and seafood, turtles, manatees and anything that could be eaten from the sea.

Homesteaders really did live off the sea in other ways, as well as being fisher-folk. They built their homes of lumber washed up from passing ships destroyed in wrecks or material washed overboard in hurricanes and storms. There was no cement in those days, but pioneers made lime by burning conch shells and other mollusks such as clamshells. No sandpaper, no problem;

they used the extremely rough skin of the triggerfish to do scrubbing chores. They made do with what they could find in their environment. In their own way, they were the original Robinson Crusoes of their day. Today, many Keys residents actually still decorate their gates and homes with flotsam and jetsam gathered on the shores from all manner of tidal-and wind-driven items from all over the world. Drive past homes today in the Keys and you will see driftwood and trap buoys festooning fences and railings of these homes, some with old rusted cannons and early channel markers, and as decoration for restaurants and gift shops.

Early settlers and pioneers planted limes, breadfruit, pineapples, melons and vegetables and had several varieties of fruits such as coconuts, sapodilla, Spanish limes and other citrus fruits. They made tea from the leaves of the lime tree. They made mattresses and filled them with soft silk grass found along the beaches. They baked sweet potato bread in outdoor brick beehive-like ovens. Homes were built on the high sand ridges along the ocean. It was said that sometimes the smell of rotting seaweed was unbearable. The early settlers were like the Indians in many ways. Most settlers never took more than they needed to survive.

The three major families that settled in the Matecumbe area were the Russells, the Pinders and the Parkers. Because of the isolation, there were few marriage choices, so many of the children married one another. Bernard Russell recalled that when he was a boy, if told to bring five lobsters or so many conchs for dinner, he was careful to bring the exact amount home. Although he could have collected hundreds of each, more than what his mother asked for would have meant trouble for him. These people had great respect for the natural bounties all around them, and it was part of their ethos not to waste anything they could use, as they might need it later and not find it again in their larder. These settlers were not tourists; they did not brag or show the bounty of the sea for macho rights—that would come much later when railroads and bridges brought outsiders. Due to their hard labor, in survival mode they weren't sport fishing either.

From the middle of the 1700s to about 1821, the Keys, on its intractable march toward our modern times, was bandied about by Spanish, British and French, but in the Treaty of Paris, Britain acquired Florida after defeating France and Spain in the Seven Years' War that ended in 1763. Spain was happy to trade off Florida. It appears that Florida had been a major aggravation to the Crown for 250 years, so in exchange for Havana, Cuba, which the British had seized and held at the time of the wars, they made a trade. Spain left Florida the way it found it—with no gold, silver or other true riches. It never tried to seriously turn Florida into anything as productive as a colony. However, when the Brits got hold of Florida, it would begin prospering nicely. The British brought numerous English Loyalists during the Revolutionary War period to Florida's northern reaches. The British had virtually no idea of the harbors, soil, fishery or climate of the east coast of Florida. They brought in Gerard de Brahm, an employee of the Board of Trade, and he, along with help of Bernard Romans, spent six years mapping South Florida and the Keys.

Romans, in a report following his work in the Keys excerpted from *Tales of Old Florida*, said:

> *Old Matacombe is remarkable for being the most handy and best watering place on the entire coast; on its east there are 5 wells in solid rock, probably cut by the savages* [Calusa Indians] *but to me they appear to be natural chasms* [wrong, they were cut by the Indians] *that yield excellent water in abundance—in-so-much, that in a wet season all the east end of the four mile key it is enough to supply the necessity of a fleet of ships. This is the key that was one of the last habitations of the savages, of the Calusa nation. About a mile to the east of the northeast end of Matacombe* [original spelling of today's Matecumbe], *lies a small bushy, gravelly key on the extremity of a reef, this key is known* [at that time] *as Matanca* [meaning "murder"] *from the catastrophe of a French boat crew said to have amounted to near three hundred men, who were unfortunate enough to fall into the hands of the Calusa, which destroyed them to a man on the spot.*

Romans, in his writings, refers to the Keys as a "heap of rocks" and says, "Matacombe alone would be worth attention of a settlement."

At the time of the British takeover, there were almost no people living in South Florida and especially in the Keys. There were perhaps only a few pirates and one or two fishermen. In 1764, a Spaniard named Juan Jose Elisio argued that the Keys were still Spanish and were not in the Spanish contract that ceded Florida to the British. However, there was nothing in the Keys worth fighting over at that time. So the Keys were just there and existed with almost no rule.

After the British lost the Revolutionary War, England had had enough. It felt that Florida was a liability and gave it back to Spain. But even though the Keys became Spanish in 1773, they were completely dominated by the Conchs of the Bahaman Islands. (Conchs were so named as they were tough and hard like the shell of the conch mollusk, a giant snail, and soft on the inside, like the snail conch meat—really kind of tough until you beat it soft). The Conchs were the tough salvagers of old and, although not necessarily pirates, were the de facto, on-the-ground governors of the Keys at that time. Florida, including the Keys, became a territory in 1821. In 1819, the Adams-Onis Treaty gave the United States title to East and West Florida, but it wasn't until 1821 that Andrew Jackson received the Floridas from Spain in Pensacola, and in March 1822, Congress created a territorial government for Florida, thus ending the 288 years of Spanish rule and the 20 years it had belonged to Britain (1763–83).

Today, when fishing around and near the Alligator Lighthouse Reef, few anglers know that piracy was so bad in the Keys and Caribbean in the early 1800s that the naval squadron sent to suppress the pirates was known as the West Indian Squadron, under the command of Commodore David Porter. The USS *Alligator* had originally been assigned to intercept slave ships. It had been built in Boston in 1820 and carried twelve cannons. It was under the command of Captain William Howard Allen. Sitting at anchor in Matanzas, Cuba, Captain Allen was told that a ship with its crew and cargo was being held for ransom by pirates in the Keys area. Allen and his crew sighted the ship on November 9, 1822. The pirates fired on the *Alligator*. Allen took two musket balls and died along with four other sailors. But the *Alligator* got the best of the pirates. It later met with disaster when it went aground on November 19, 1822. The ship could not be freed and, after being stripped, was burned to prevent pirates from taking anything of use from the ship. Today, the aforementioned Alligator Light off Islamorada Key is a fine fish-aggregating lighthouse that sits on the area where the old *Alligator* came to ruin.

There were numerous deep coves and inlets and various hidden harbors to protect pirates from being seen until they were able to make their sneak attacks. Note that these hidden harbors, coves and inlets today are mostly the same wild places they were in the past. Why? Mangroves protect them from being developed. Basically, only tales are documented, as the pirates left little history of their exploits and presence in the Florida Keys. Just south and east of Islamorada lies Indian Key. I've visited this eleven-acre island many times over the past forty years. Also, just over today's Overseas Highway, out in the Gulf of Mexico (Florida Bay area) about two miles, lies Lignum Vitae Key, a biologist's mecca. This small island has various creatures found nowhere else in the Keys. Today, it is visited by tourists wanting to view the way the Keys appeared in the past.

Chapter 3

Fishing Methods and
Travels to the Keys

B y the time Karl Benz patented his Motorwagen, a mom and pop auto operation with his sons pitching in too, the Vom Hofe brothers, also in Germany, had begun offering a fishing reel that, in the late 1800s, was as revolutionary as Benz's ten-mile-per-hour, three-wheeled motorized wagon, the precursor of what we know today as the Mercedes Benz. Before the Industrial Revolution, there were clock makers that understood gears, wheels and the fine mechanics of small moving parts. A few of them, like the Vom Hofes, made excellent German silver reels that were based on the gearing of their clocks. The first reels were made for friends, and then, as the popularity of their reels grew based on word of mouth, they tried their hand at a whole new industry—making a variety of fly, bass and big-game reels. In turn, there were the Pfluegers, the Meeks and Milams, but as far as Keys saltwater reels at the turn of the century, Vom Hofes were considered the best.

From the 1800s to the present, the exploration and evolution of both fishing techniques and conservation efforts to protect the habitats of this maritime reef environment have basically been hit and miss revolutions. In the 1800s, all travel to the Keys was accomplished by sailing craft. With the exception of eating the fish caught on fishing trips, everything else had to be brought with the travelers. Yes, there were freshwater wells in the Matecumbe islands (no bridges yet), but for safe water to be ensured, freshwater had to be brought along for the trip.

Before commercial fishing rods and reels, pronged spears, hand lines and nets were cast for fish, early horsehair linen lines and catgut leaders were

Line winder and other early gear and tackle from the turn of the nineteenth and twentieth centuries. The roller line dryer was part of the arsenal of an experienced angler used to dry his or her linen line after wash-cleansing from salt water. *Courtesy of the IGFA, photo by author at IGFA Library.*

tied to bamboo or wood sticks with hooks and bait. Early rods and reels were rudimentary at best for the strong, swift fish that this gear would be called upon to tackle. Basically, what had been built for fresh water was used in salt water for animals that were far swifter and more powerful than any freshwater fish. Freshwater fish do not have to fight tides and sharks. The linen lines had to be freshwater cleansed and then dried after each day of use on a line winder. This let the lines dry overnight. Reels had no star adjustable drags, but they did have leather thumb pressure pads that allowed an angler to use his thumb to slow down the speed of the rotating reel spool. When a fish ran, many a tale was told of that friction-burned thumb that throbbed over dinner and during sleep.

Rods were nothing like today's engineered wonders of modern fiberglass and carbon fiber. Rods of the past were of boxwood, bamboo and steel; they were heavy, and they warped. When lines ran through the guides, they wore grooves that caused lines to fray and break when heavy pressure was put on them by strong fish pulling and gyrating in the air, as in a tarpon fight. There were no stainless hooks on lures or leaders, so rust was a factor, and hooks needed to be sharpened frequently to be able to penetrate the bony mouths of Keys fishing denizens of the deep and shallows. Reels often were taped to rods, as reel seats, after just one season, rusted and corroded away.

When DuPont came upon the formula for Dacron, this was a giant leap into a new product that could handle the severe beating fishing lines take when fished in salt water. Later still, in the 1940s and '50s, monofilament revolutionized the entire fishing industry. Here was a fishing line that could be made in multiple weight classes, was clear and fooled wary fish more easily than any other line in history—and it stretched. This line does not need a drying wheel and can be used on any fishing reel. However, "mono" was really made for the relatively new types of reels that did not require a revolving spool—the spinning reel! Monofilament line is pulled by the weight of the lure; it coils off a vertical spool that doesn't move at all. The spring-loaded wire bail drops down, and the line is instantly picked up by a specially designed pickup bail. These reels pick up line at a three-to-one or four-to-one ratio, have ball bearings and are smooth and serviceable fishing tools. The big deal with a spinning reel is that there are few or no "bird's nests" and tangled lines from over rolling conventional spools when they are cast.

From the 1840s, all manner of hand-made wood, balsa and metallic lures were being made. (Note that at an auction of sporting memorabilia in Kennebunkport, Maine, a mile from President Bush's home, I saw one of those metal lures stamped "1848" sell for $22,000.) Live baits were dried; cut baits were placed in alcohol-filled bottles and sold at some apothecary shops. It was the dawning of a revolution whose niche would be filled by the Heddons, Pfluegers and a variety—actually, a huge variety—of lures coming from many dozen makers across the United States and Europe.

Sport fishing was coming of age. Mass production would eventually come to the Eppingers (the famous Flatfish lure that took the freshwater fishing scene by storm), the red and white Daredevil and, in Europe, from Norway and still going strong today, the Rapala balsa lure, to name but a few of the greats. Fishing reels had names like Pflueger President, the Mitchell CAP (made in France), the Mitchell 300 and Shakespeare; even Sears got into the reel business and named its spinning reels, made in Italy, the Ted Williams, one of the first to connect baseball with fishing. The big name in big game was and is Penn. It offered an entire lineup of gold reels called Internationals, in sizes and gear ratios to handle any size fish that swims. Another of the well-known companies that were and are top-of-the-line in offshore fishing reels is Tycoon Fin-Nor. It was the rage in the early days of offshore fishing, and it's no wonder—these reels are lifetime-quality, hand-me-down heritage products. I have a 5/0, and it's not for sale; even though it's fifty years old, it can still help hoist a giant out of the sea.

Chapter 4

Fishing Guides and Their Exploits

When talking about fishing guides of the past, some call them legendary. I call many that, too, but this book is not about all of them. (I'll let others write that book.) However, there were and are guides—fortunately, many still alive, fishing and kicking just fine—who need to be mentioned along with the life's trade they have chosen. Many of the early guides got into the business when the railroad was finished and the roads were put in. Many worked on the roads and railroad, and most gravitated to becoming commercial fishermen, catching turtles, working on finding and selling sponges and catching barrels of mackerel. When their businesses dried up and they were asked to take visitors fishing, some did so. These early guides soon realized that taking a customer fishing was a much better and easier way to make a living than commercial fishing. Often, they would build a little cabin and offer their fares a place to sleep. Their wives would cook some fish, and *Voila!*, they were in the tourist business. A few of them tweaked their fishing businesses and developed them over time to become highly successful enterprises (one guide I know takes in $175,000 per year, but he also works seven days per week and gets up at four o'clock in the morning every day he sails). The popularity of sport fishing mirrors in many ways the success of the industrial revolution. As people had more free time after the transition from seven-day-a-week farming situations to city jobs and vocations, there was more time off to enjoy recreational pursuits, and they had some money to spend on quality new fishing gear, too.

Guides who have learned the waters of the Keys were and still are a good bet for any visitor. Most guides have already spent many years understanding the fish, the tides, the currents, baits and, most importantly, where to find the fish. In my thirty years in the Keys, I have been asked by newcomers, some here for just a day or two as tourist anglers and some who have just moved to the Keys, whether they should hire a guide. My frequent retort was: "Are you a plumber?" "Well, no," came the answer. "Well," I'd say, "would you do your own plumbing repairs? Do you have the tools and knowledge? Are you willing to waste your time and money trying to learn the plumbing business so that you can do your own plumbing the right way, without springing leaks and stripping faucets and burning down your bathroom with a blow torch?" Always the answer would be "No." "Well then, why do you want to reinvent the wheel by going out fishing without good knowledge of the five W's—where, what, when, why and with whom—and very importantly, how?"

I've fished with dozens of guides and big boat captains from Key West to Key Largo, and one guide who stands out for me is Captain Adler of the *Kalex*. The *Kalex* is berthed at Bud N' Mary's Fishing Marina in Islamorada. One of my trips with Adler was for king mackerel. His mate tossed a cast net at a silvery pod of pilchard baitfish. The bait well was soon filled, and we were off, trolling four twelve-inch ballyhoo, used more as teasers than actual hooked-up baits—two fish from flat lines that extend back from the boat on clips at the gunnels (flat off the boat's gunnels) and two baits from outriggers that help dance the baits over the waves and ocean foam. We were out seven miles, parallel to the island of Islamorada. We had strikes, brought in a couple king mackerel and found the schooling fish. Then we began a slow-drift troll with swimming pilchards. Many pilchards were thrown over the side to attract the schooling kingfish and bring them up from the depths to hopefully strike our baits. Captain Adler told his mate that one of the hooked baits he looked at from the tower wasn't swimming correctly. "This bait won't get struck!" he yelled out over the drone of the diesel engine. The mate began arguing that he felt it would and Alex was wrong. After ten more minutes, nothing struck. Alex said, "Change that bait, and let me see it swim." The mate finally did change the bait, and not more than ten seconds later, a kingfish struck it. Alex didn't say a thing; he didn't gloat. We just went on fishing, and privately Alex told me that even the slightest thing can determine if a game fish will or will not strike. Alex spent his life learning from his dad and personal experience what those slightest things were, and today—and for the past forty years—he is booked more than about any other charter boat in the Keys.

Adler was found by Johnny Morris to be a fabulous tuna captain, and he has assisted Morris, owner of the Bass Pro dynasty, to be a winner in large tournament events in the Bahamas and elsewhere around the world. I believe Adler thinks like the fish do—I'm sure of it! His saying, which I often repeat to other erstwhile anglers who tell me they are going to catch this fish or that on their outing, is: "Never fish the fish; always fish the conditions." This has proven to be correct on almost all of my fishing trips and remains the one big reason he has so many repeat angler-customer-friends today. Alex's secret in how he has been able to be booked most of the year, every year, for his charter boat business: "I keep a log. I always make sure to write in all information about every trip; tides, weather and current conditions, bait used, fish caught and who I fished and how well they did or didn't. After forty years, you get to see the connections. You find that experience that only time allows. My trick is to find that edge, keep sharpening it and being as close to the fish I target and the conditions needed to catch them as if I am one of them myself."

My personal favorite artificial baits were made by Walt and Millie Garretson of Grassy Key, who have passed on now. They made the most successful buck tail jigs between New York, Key West and Maine. Their little Keys cottage industry relied on deer tails for their jigs, which they basically colored red and white. These buck tails were lollipops to snook and other inshore predators. The hollow hair of the deer tail fluttered and gave the jig a lifelike look. Their lures are still being sold today, but the quaint and delightfully friendly couple, who drove Millies Bucktails off the Keys each year to sell the lures to tackle shops up and down the Atlantic coast, added to the feel of what the old Keys was all about: mom and pop entrepreneurship at its finest, from a pioneering, ever-evolving, once-wild, very fishy place in the world—the Florida Keys.

I caught my first snook in the Keys on a Millies and went on to stock several in my tackle box. Before artificial fibers, most lures used natural hairs and even whalebone to make jigs.

Chapter 5

Private and Governmental Programs

The Florida Keys are so popular today that they were and still are in danger of being loved to death. The concerns are maintaining the quality of clear water, proper sewage drainage, amount of damage to reefs by anchors and overfishing reefs and all the waters that surround and brush by the Keys, in tide and Gulf Stream. Millions of people worldwide know the delicate chain of islands, or keys, extending from the southern tip of Florida, but far too often they don't recognize that this ecosystem is extremely sensitive to degradation and destruction of all those things that make the Keys so spectacular.

The "golden goose" is internationally regarded as a tropical paradise, and yet, like Yellowstone National Park, which was and is in great danger of full-on destruction of its habitats, wildlife and other natural resources, laws and protection are necessary to ensure the future of this and other overused and loved places. So it is with the waters surrounding the Florida Keys, long appreciated for their unique beauty and the abundance of marine life they support. Congressional leaders felt the same way when, in 1990, they designated these waters as a 2,900-nautical-square-mile marine sanctuary, and President Bush, on November 16, 1990, signed the law into being. However, even before 1990, the Key Largo and Looe Key National Marine Sanctuaries were established in 1975 and 1981, respectively, and then they, too, were incorporated into the new Florida Keys National Marine Sanctuary Management plan of 1990.

The perception by Congress was mainly attributed not to the islands themselves but to the clear, shallow waters surrounding them. These warm tropical waters are also known today as the Florida Keys National Marine Sanctuary (FKNMS). The Florida Keys and its marine environment offer unparalleled beauty and diversity. The entire Keys chain is teeming with thousands of colorful tropical fish, marine invertebrates and plants. The waters of the Florida Keys are home to the world's third-largest barrier coral reef system, thousands of acres of sea grasses and hundreds of miles of mangrove-fringed shoreline. The special beauty of the Florida Keys National Marine Sanctuary brings with it some unique challenges for protection. Every year, more than two and a half million people come to the Keys to experience the wonders of the waters. Year round, visitors and residents alike dive, snorkel, fish, boat and swim in these waters. A system of mooring buoys, channel markers and special marine zones is in place today to ensure that the diverse and delicate ecosystem of the Florida Keys National Marine Sanctuary remains healthy for generations to come. Just imagine how much damage an anchor does on a reef and multiply this thousands of times over.

After much public input, a Comprehensive Management Plan was developed, and sanctuary regulations went into effect on July 1, 1997. The revised management plan went into effect in December 2007. The sanctuary is located in Monroe County's nearby towns and cities of Florida Keys, Key West, Marathon and Key Largo. The FKNMS encompasses 3,801 square miles of protected area consisting of the waters surrounding the archipelago formed by the Florida Keys, which includes waters of Florida Bay, the Gulf of Mexico and the Atlantic Ocean. The Florida Keys National Marine Sanctuary is at the conflux of three watersheds. First, the Mississippi River watershed drains 40 percent of the continental United States. The Mississippi River eventually drains down into the Gulf of Mexico, where those waters are picked up by the Loop Current, which passes the Florida Keys as it merges with the Florida Current (Gulf Stream). (Note that this was why BP's giant oil spill was so damaging. It was damaging in tourist perception and to the waterway's ecosystem—"Everyone lives downstream.") Second, the Florida Bay and the Florida Keys are the end recipients of the Kissimmee Okeechobee Everglades (KOE) watershed, which drains much of the state of Florida. The third watershed affecting the waters of the Keys originates in the Caribbean, where the waters draining to the ocean are funneled through the Yucatan straight and eventually merge with the Florida Current (Gulf Stream). (This information was partially taken from the FKNMS Management Plan.)

Keys Habitat

Although the best-known feature of the Keys marine environment is its coral reefs, the shallow waters near the shore are actually composed of a series of interconnecting and interdependent natural habitats. These include fringing mangroves and sea grass meadows, as well as hard-bottom regions, patch reefs and bank reefs. When healthy, the communities of mangroves, sea grasses and corals protect and enhance one another. Upland, hardwood hammocks are equally important; they protect the soil from erosion while their decaying vegetation provides necessary nutrients to the mangrove and sea grass communities. In turn, mangroves, sea grass beds and coral reefs serve as self-repairing breakwaters to protect the hammocks—and the rest of the Keys—by absorbing the force of the waves.

Fringing mangroves filter material washed from the land, trapping debris and sediment. The remains of plants and animals are broken down into nutrients by bacteria and fungi. Mangrove roots provide nursery grounds to many species of fish and invertebrates. Mangrove forests near North Key Largo also are habitats for the endangered American crocodile.

Sea grass meadows grow in much of Florida Bay and the shallow waters seaward out to the reef line. They are a natural trap for sediment. The predominant turtle grasses, which happen to be particularly vulnerable to pollution, are nursery and feeding grounds for a host of attaching invertebrates and for the larvae and young of many organisms. These include shrimp, spiny lobster, sea urchins, sponges, snapper, sea trout, barracuda and grunts. Adult fish from the reefs often feed among the sea grasses, and endangered species of green sea turtles and manatees browse there regularly.

The Florida reef tract is the most extensive living coral reef system in North American waters and the third-largest reef system in the world. It provides habitat, refuge and feeding grounds for countless colorful and exotic creatures. Colonies of tiny polyps form the complex structure of coral reefs by secreting calcium carbonate. The waving forests of sea whips and sea fans in the Keys are a uniquely Caribbean feature and are not found on reefs in the Pacific and Indian Oceans. (This information comes from the FKNMS Management Plan.)

Fortunately, the State of Florida and the federal government have been working together for about forty years to protect the marine environment in the Florida Keys. The fourteen action plans within the FKNMS Management Plan include: Science Management and Administration, Waterway Management, Education/Outreach, Enforcement, Mooring

Buoys, Regulatory, Research and Monitoring, Maritime Heritage Resources, Damage Assessment and Restoration, Water Quality, Operations, Evaluation, Volunteer and Marine Zoning.

Having lived in the Keys for more than thirty years, I saw how publicizing the Keys caused its great fishing, diving, lobstering and shrimping during winter months to degrade. Other issues like collecting reef material for the aquarium trade, filling coolers with dolphin, captains selling their catches made during sport fishing charters and just about any unregulated way to exploit the natural resources was seriously degrading what the Keys had to offer. During one lobster weekend, I observed, as fishing editor for the *Miami Herald*, car checks being made at the Islamorada truck checking station. These random checks found nearly every checked vehicle heading back to the mainland with one or more illegal violations of the marine laws. Officers found undersize and female lobsters with eggs, undersize groupers and snappers, tiny speared fish, coral chunks and bags of tropical reef fish for aquariums. Officers of the Marine Patrol told me if they had the manpower and could stop each and every vehicle without stopping traffic for miles, I would be astounded at how many people were far more than scoffing the laws during their trips to the Keys. In previous years, I recall the times I wrote about those incidents of legal lobster traps being raided by thieves. Lots of harsh lessons learned by would-be thieves have cut down this problem to near zero today. The Keys really had rules closer to the Old West way of doing things. I observed some of these during the 1970s.

Chapter 6

A Special Captain and a Unique Lifelong Fossil Hunter

Captain Bob Lewis, fishing captain for Bob Knight of the *Miami Herald* newspaper group, could have rightfully bragged about his major fishing exploits and his fishing kite that brought very strong interest worldwide to fishing in South Florida and the Keys. Captain Bob didn't brag. Bob Lewis, captain of the first hovercraft used in the U.S. Navy, was also an officer for the Miami Police Department. Lewis went to Glasgow, Scotland, to be trained in how to run America's first navy hovercraft. He captained the craft at the Key West Naval Station. Lewis had many true tales to tell about his charters and other fishing exploits from the 1940s until his passing in 1999, and the Lewis name was prominent in the skies over the Gulf Stream, made famous by being emblazoned on his manufactured fishing kite (I have an original kite hanging in my office). He was credited with bringing the fishing kite to Florida's fishing community, as well as other American coastal fishing areas. Lewis began manufacturing kites and kite reels in the 1950s, and throughout the Keys, just about every charter boat began using them.

Captain Bob told me one interesting story of how, in the 1940s, he used to go down to the old abutments left over from the railroad, on which much of the Overseas Highway was built, to catch jewfish (today called goliath grouper). He would bring them back in his Model-A Ford to a Miami fish house and would be paid two cents a pound. One trip, he said, had his truck pitted against a 550-pound fish, and after hooking it up on a sisal rope in the Upper Keys area, he dragged it out and over a boat ramp near the bridge to an incline so he could have some height leverage to get it into the pickup box. Nevertheless, he was alone and had a very hard time getting the fish into the pickup. However, Lewis himself was a big, tough customer and managed the job, knowing it would be a good week's pay for him. As he drove toward Miami, the fish bounced around and, still alive, managed to flop itself out of the pickup truck bed. He tried very hard to get the fish back into the truck but just couldn't. He sat down alongside the fish for an hour in the middle of the road. Eventually, he spotted a gasoline truck, the only vehicle he saw during that time, and the driver helped him get the fish loaded again. He did sell the fish and said that he took the next week off.

I could fill a book with the tales told to me by Captain Lewis before he went to his happy fishing grounds in the sky. He went fishing again eight years before his passing after a double lung and heart transplant (his church raised $800,000; he had no insurance). They don't make them like Captain Lewis anymore.

Another friend, Vito Bertucci, visited me in the Keys and showed me something that was truly jaw-dropping: at eleven feet wide and over eight feet tall, the world's largest set of shark jaws composed of 182 fossil teeth. These were later sold at the Heritage Auction Galleries in Texas. This huge prehistoric jaw (the fossilized teeth part) once belonged to a megalodon shark, the largest predatory shark ever to have existed on our planet. It took late fossil hunter Bertucci more than sixteen years to assemble this piece with fossilized tooth specimens of the appropriate size and shape. Bertucci personally collected most of the specimens in the coastal rivers of South Carolina. Megalodon had ruled the oceans and the marine food chain for almost twenty million years. The megalodon could exceed one hundred feet in length and had teeth seven inches across and nine inches long. The largest jaw set in the world also contains four teeth that measure over nine inches each along the diagonal. The asking price for the world's largest shark's jaw was $650,000. The auction house expected it to sell for $700,000 and up. Bertucci told me it sold for over $1 million. He also showed me the smaller jaw he was selling to a museum in Rhode Island; he told me a few months after the sale the big jaw went to the Museum of Natural History in New York. The smaller jaw would be sold to Rhode Island for about $700,000. Over the years, he gave me a few teeth that were over six inches long, and I treasure them today as his legacy.

My friend Vito Bertucci was forty-eight years old and from Port Royal. He went diving in the Ogeechee River near the Intracoastal Waterway in Bryan County at about 2:30 p.m. one day and told his partner he would surface in about ten minutes. After nearly a week of searching, the Bryan County

Sheriff's Office says a fisherman discovered the body of Vito, known as the "Megalodon Man," when it surfaced in Ossabaw Sound in Chatham County. It was reported that he had a heart attack. I think he got stuck in a snag in the chocolate water and drowned. He always told me how dangerous it was, and he unfortunately proved himself correct.

Chapter 7

Fish Preparation, Recipes and Preservation

The early inhabitants probably had several ways they preserved food, but there is little evidence—with the exception of pottery shards that held various foodstuffs. However, it is known from early drawings by Spanish visitors depicting life in early Indian villages in the Keys that they sun-dried fish on racks, and since there was no refrigeration, and due to the ease of creating salt by drying sea water, many foods were salted for preservation. However, little preservation was necessary as fresh fish and seafood were everywhere in Keys waters. There is little evidence of the Indians growing produce; however, it is a well-known fact that early settlers cultivated bananas, pineapples, tomatoes and other crops by using seaweed and natural mulches from the rotten leaves of the forests and jungle. Later on, as in the rest of the country, glass-jar canning was used for certain vegetables. Due to the incredible humidity, and the fact that root cellars were virtually impossible to dig due to the high water table and coral rock, the most likely preservation methods were marinating fish and other seafood. Still, fresh was best, so most of the food from the sea was caught, cleaned and prepared for the table the same day.

Ceviche, also spelled *cebiche* or *seviche*, is a traditional Spanish dish. It is typically made from fresh raw fish, conch meat, Florida lobster, shrimp and other seafood marinated in citrus juices, such as lemon or lime, and spiced with chili peppers. Great additional seasonings, such as chopped onions and salt, were also added. Ceviche is usually accompanied by side dishes that complement its flavors, such as sweet potato, plantain, lettuce, corn and avocado. As the dish is not cooked with heat, it's usually eaten soon after it is prepared. It was probably introduced to the Keys by the Spaniards; they also introduced the limes for which the Keys are noted today. Nowadays, ceviche is a popular international dish prepared in a variety of ways throughout the Americas, the Caribbean and other nations of the tropics.

Vinegar was a valuable commodity, as was sugar. Ice came to the Keys only when the railroad began operation in 1912, and it was expensive. Ice was carried on ferries, and blocks were sold to businesses needing it in the Keys. Lobsters were taken only when needed. Turtles and manatees were butchered for fresh meat, and there were deer and boar to be hunted. Roasting and stewing over open fires and coals was the rule in the olden days—no fried conch fritters as far as we know. A favorite dish that was often eaten by original settlers and well into the middle of the twentieth century was grits and grunts. The protein-rich and easy-to-catch grunts right off the dock or rocks, together with the starch of grits, made a healthy, inexpensive meal. Roasted over the fire, pan friend or stewed, this fish and grits combo was, by virtue of the conditions in the Keys, an excellent food source.

The following recipe, titled "Hurricane Shrimp," from my book *Calypso Café*, is a wonderful way to prepare the most famous and tasty crustacean found in Keys waters. It will make a dish that would more than satisfy three to four diners:

1 pound (11 to 15 count) white or pink shrimp, peeled and deveined
1 tablespoon coarse salt
1 tablespoon fresh thyme
2 cloves garlic, sliced fine
Pinch of crushed red pepper flakes
Pinch of cayenne pepper
Juice of 2 Key limes
1 teaspoon black pepper

Place the shrimp and salt in an ice water bath while preparing the marinade. Mix the thyme and remaining 5 ingredients in a blender or food processor. Drain the shrimp. Combine shrimp and thyme mixture and marinate for at least 30 minutes. Broil the shrimp on a barbecue or in an oven for 10 minutes or until done. Add pasta or rice, a favorite veggie and "mangia" with a big smile.

Chapter 8

The Ubiquitous Key Lime Pie and Famous Florida Lobster

The key lime pie is now so famous that just about every restaurant offers it as a favored after-dinner dessert treat. However, as the name says, "Lime," far too many pies come out of the kitchen colored various shades of green, utilizing food colors that a paint store would offer. Key limes were originally brought in from Spain. The key lime is a small, round lime that appears to be a lemon, as its color is yellow when ripe. Today, the lime tree is found in most back and front yards of Florida Keys homes. The true key to a real key lime pie is this generally mellow, yellow, lemon-lime fruit. The key lime pie was a popular dessert of the Bahamians, who originally held great sway in the Keys in their business ventures of wrecking, turtling, fishing and other industries. Sweetened condensed canned milk that did not need refrigeration, crushed graham cracker crust (likewise no refrigeration), sugar, a bit of cream of tartar, eggs and *Voila!*, you have key lime pie.

So many stories abound about who made the first key lime pie offered to visitors, but one in particular stands out. The Curry Mansion, owned by the Curry family, had a cook named Aunt Sally. She presented this pie to the family and their visitors in 1894. The best key lime pie that brought locals and visitors alike to their doors was found at the restaurant owned and operated by Manny and Isa. Isa picked the limes from her backyard trees and basically offered the same recipe used by Aunt Sally back before the 1900s. The following is that recipe, which I received from Edith Amsterdam, an owner of the Curry Mansion Inn in Key West:

4 eggs, separated
½ cup key lime juice
1 can (14-ounces) sweetened condensed milk
1 (8-inch) graham cracker crust
¼ teaspoon cream of tartar
⅓ cup sugar
Thin slices of lime for garnish

Beat the egg yolks until thick and lemon colored. Blend in the lime juice. Stir in milk until mixture thickens. Pour mixture into crust. Beat egg whites and cream of tartar until stiff. Gradually mix in sugar, beating until glossy peaks form. Spread over pie to the edge of the crust. Bake at 350 degrees for 20 minutes or until golden brown. Chill and garnish. Serves 8.

There are many tasty variations that use burnt almonds and other ingredients. Jimmy Buffett's Margaritaville Café in Key West has virtually the same recipe, but somehow it's more fun to eat there as there is great people watching available at this restaurant. In the old days, the pie wasn't kept around enough to spoil due to lack of refrigeration—yes, it's that good! After having a true piece of this pie—light and fluffy with fresh limes—you'll see why, after getting off your charter skiff or boat, you'll want to head straight to a Keys restaurant for this treat.

Florida lobster? The Florida lobster, so much in demand today, was once nearly as prolific as mosquitoes. The Florida lobster is really a giant crawfish and has no claws like the cold-water species of true lobster found along the northeastern seaboard from Massachusetts, along the entire Maine Coast and up into the maritime provinces of Canada. In the past, and even today, Florida lobsters were used as live and cut bait for big grouper, cubera snapper and other reef fish.

When I first came to the Keys in the early 1970s, all I had to do was basically reach down, dip a net and "tickle" a nice fat lobster into it anytime I wanted to. For many years since, there has been a lobster two-day free-for-all of locals (mostly recent locals) and visitors who bring their tickle sticks and whole families to fill their bag-limits of these tasty—albeit, except for their tails, mostly wasted—crustaceans. An entire commercial fishery has been in existence for many decades to supply Florida restaurants with lobster tails. No longer can you just go and easily find your own fresh lobster and ring its tail for dinner. Today, it's "dive baby, dive," and just in the right spot—perhaps at a sunken barrel or concrete culvert purposely sunk in some hidden spot, only known by the sinker. It's not legal to take females or shorts (shorts are under limit–sized tails).

Chapter 9

Industrial Art in Fishing Rods over the Past 120 Years

R ods in the past were made of wood, steel and bamboo. But first lines were cast without rods altogether. In the Keys, this was known as the "Cuban hand line method of fishing." Line was swung around and around, and the weight of the baited hook, with or without any other weights, when thrown and released would sail out toward the fishy waters. Hand lines were and are great for yellowtail fishing, and commercial fishermen used this method because it is quicker, easier and allowed more fish to come over the gunnels than other methods. I tried this when I first arrived in the Keys, and it worked very well.

As far as rods were concerned, wood warps and steel rusts and is heavy, with little sensitivity, when a fish is struck. Bamboo rods were costly in time and experience to make properly, and they too warped, came apart from moisture and humidity and could develop mold from the glues that were used (horse products), so they needed real care before and after each use in fresh- and certainly saltwater environs. Rods of the past were heavier than anything made today, and they are now part of the fishing memorabilia collections of thousands of collectors and museums. This, of course, goes for anything fishing hundreds of years ago or even seventy-five years ago.

The evolution of rods is parallel to other equipment used in sport and the building trades. We all know how a Model-A was a strongly built automobile: heavier metals, rubber wheels, engine blocks, forty-mile-per-hour capacity. Today, vehicles made of carbon fibers go over two hundred miles per hour. Carbon fiber is king! When fiberglass was developed, rods were still heavier than today, but they didn't warp, were lighter than wood and bamboo and bent beautifully in a smooth, parabolic arc that didn't break as easily as all other rods before them. These, in turn, were overshadowed by today's mandrill-spun graphite fiber rods; light, strong, straight and reasonably priced, they handle all weather and humidity conditions, and they store and even break down in sections, making them a smaller package to travel with.

As the Florida Keys has very high humidity much of the year and especially during the summer and early fall months, you don't find many collectible early rods in the Keys. They have long gone down the road of the early boats and anything in the saltwater environment. Lures and hooks are rusted out and paints faded or cracked from the harsh climate. Old fishing books would have been better kept somewhere other than in the Keys—books warped, pages turned brown and dried out, water marks appeared, ink faded or even ran. When fiberglass came along (my first rod was bought in Brooklyn, New York, in 1954), my uncle Sid also got me my reel, a Mitchell 300-spin reel that I still have today, but the guides rusted off the rod, and a striped bass helped splinter the rod on a powerful run with my drag tightened down too much. Today, as millions of other anglers have found, graphite is king for all manner and all sizes and weights of fishing rods. Shakespeare (virtually unbreakable Ugly Stick Is King), Pflueger, Fenwick, Penn, Wright & McGill (Eagle Claw) Daiwa, Orvis, Shimano, Fin-Nor—originally, the highest-quality reels for saltwater anglers, they now offer their own named branded rods as well.

There are numerous other rod manufacturers today, a great amount coming in from foreign countries, and many others came and went over the past 120 years, but the ones mentioned here are generally those most often purchased. There is a great cottage industry, too. Randy Towe in the Florida Keys makes excellent fishing rods to order. They are all personalized, and there are other great cottage crafters of fine rods all over the United States.

Today, many anglers want to jump up from conventional rods that use drum wheel reels and spinning reels to fly-fishing gear, capable of hooking and holding almost every saltwater fish (with the exception of a large yellow fin tuna). The awesome tarpon, truly the silver king, is now regularly caught and released by heavier saltwater fly rods, wielded by sportsters who make pilgrimages to the Keys and other tropical waters to test their mettle on this steel-muscled fish. All inshore fish such as sea trout, snook, permit and bonefish are tackled by lighter rod wielders, and it is truly great fun, as you can make several false casts, as well as fast direct casts, to reach a sight-fished

Captain Randy Towe was the first guide to assist the author with fishing opportunities for his articles about the Florida Keys for the *Miami Herald*. Captain Towe makes custom fishing rods at his shop in Islamorada and takes anglers fishing as a guide for inshore fish, such as this tarpon, and offshore fish, such as all of the billfish clan that ply the waters of the Gulf Stream. *Courtesy of Captain Randy Towe.*

quarry. Every cast by bait cast–type reels or spin reels has to be reeled back, and that takes a bit of time; with the fly rod, numerous casts to a rising and feeding fish can be made. Of course, for trout and other freshwater fish, fly-fishing was that special sport of landed gentry in Europe for at least three hundred years or more. But fly-fishing for large saltwater fish is really relatively new in the United States.

My boys and I did a test fishing for feeding sea trout that were on the move. I was able to get off four casts to every one my sons could make with spinning tackle. When we used the fly rod, we could present custom-made or store-bought streamers and hook and hold fish three or four to one over use of the spinning reel outfits. It was and is great fun! With the development of stainless steel and tungsten guides, carefully designed and engineered lighter-weight but strong tapered rods and reel seats that do not degrade and corrode by touching two dissimilar metals left in storage, fishing gear has come a long way. Today, a fast, soft wash-off of saltwater spray on line, reel and rod is the rule. In the past, everything had to be taken down, cleaned

This display depicts Stu Apte and Bill Smith, along with two other guides who specialized in bonefish and permit fishing. Tarpon, too, of course! *Courtesy of the author, photo taken at the IGFA Library.*

individually, line-dried on a roller, the reel oiled and wiped and rods carefully cleaned and put away in a cloth sleeve and rod holder while one hoped no mold grew on the lacquered guides when stored. It was a different story. But I still do a thorough cleaning of my gear—it's a good habit.

Chapter 10

Bud N' Mary's Fishing Marina and My Fishing Experiences

Bud N' Mary's (B&M) Fishing Marina is the only fishing marina that has been in continual operation since World War II in the Upper Keys and all the way to Key West.

For more than thirty years, I fished out of Bud N' Mary's Fishing Marina, both offshore and inshore, mainly on the *Catch 22*, a fifty-five-foot Carolina-built boat captained by Scott Stanczyk. His brother, Richard Stanczyk, owned Bud N' Mary's and recently turned the business over to his children, Nick and Rick Stanczyk. They are both now fishing guides and captains in their own right, and might I add, being brought up from toddlers at the marina, they learned to be very good fishermen. Captain Richard Stanczyk knows bonefish, tarpon, sailfish and tuna on conventional and spin gear, as well as the fly rod, and for the past eleven years, along with Scott and son Nick, he has pioneered daytime swordfishing.

Legendary guides and the rich and famous have fished out of B&M for more than seventy years. More MET (Metropolitan Miami and South Florida Fishing Tournament) and IGFA records have been caught out of B&M than probably any other marina in the Keys. A few of the world-renowned guides who worked out of Bud N' Mary's are Captain Buddy Grace, Jimmy Albright and Captain Jack Brothers. I fished with them, and many of my early fishing images were made off their boats.

I had a fishing museum set up at Bud N' Mary's in what is now its dive shop location and met many anglers coming to fish with their favorite and assigned guides. What I always heard was that they opted to fish out of

Left: This image is of Captain Tom Johnson showing off his over 250-pound tarpon. The length was over seven feet, and it was caught in the author's backyard in Tavernier Bay. *Photo courtesy of IGFA.*

Below: Irving Eyster and family on a boating excursion around Islamorada. Eyster and family enjoy taking a boat ride out of Bud N' Mary's Fishing Marina to Indian Key and Lignum Vitae Key Islands, only visited by boat. *Courtesy of the author.*

Captain Buddy Grace, at Bud N' Mary's, showing off his client's tarpon. Captain Grace was a fixture on fishing docks for more than half a century. *Courtesy of historian Irving Eyster.*

B&M because they were always successful there. "There is no substitute for professional captains and guides," they all told me. I would be remiss in not saying that today absolutely all marinas have professional captains and guides in the Keys. I fished with many of them but cannot include everyone in this book—there's just not enough room.

The following sections are excerpts from two of my articles published about my experiences fishing out of Bud N' Mary's Fishing Marina.

Cobia on the Fly

An early morning haze with promise of another clear, high-sun day in the Florida Keys greeted us at the dock just before we left for Hawks Channel, a few miles offshore of Islamorada in the Atlantic. The *Catch 22* charter boat was on a mission to catch cobia on a fly. We were after nature's special rough-and-tumble tough creature—the cobia—and we were going to do it with a fly rod. Cobia go by several different names in Florida and around the world. They are called lemon fish, cabeo, ling, black salmon, black kingfish, sergeant fish, crab eater, runner. They are large, powerful fish, but all have one thing in common: they are dumb as rocks. That is, until you hook a big one, and it then heads for the cover of reef or rock to cut you off. Adult cobia, according to the *IGFA World Record Game Fishes* book, prefer shallow continental shelf waters that are in tropical and warm temperate waters. However, you can find cobia just offshore. These fish like buoys, wrecks, pilings, flotsam and jetsam and anchored boats, and they will sometimes concentrate around these objects.

I remember my first Key West party boat experience in 1973. My wife and boys were fishing in Key West on a party boat for kingfish, and about a fifty-pound cobia swam right up on the surface and cruised around the boat within a spinning rod's length of the rails. The mate yelled for the rail-huggers to drop bait to the fish. He saw dollar signs, money on the hoof and fin. He did not wait for someone to oblige with a bait to the fish and free-gaffed it into the boat, yelling all the time that this was his fish. Actually, he thought the fish would leave quickly and did not have any patience for us paying customers at all. But that was a long time ago. That mate is no longer with that boat—or any other, I'm told (who knows, he may have been pulled overboard by another larger fish he free-gaffed).

Aboard the *Catch-22* was Vic Gaspenny, a fine backcountry guide on a busman's holiday; Richard Stanczyk, owner of Bud 'N Mary's Marina in Islamorada; and me. The *Catch 22* was captained by Scott Stanczyk and his mate, Jose. We temporarily heaved to in the shallows, finding large schools of pilchards. We caught hundreds of pilchards (little silver baits that looked like shiny shards of glass in the new, once-in-a-lifetime early morning sun) for live chum and baits. They were used for those aboard who wished to fish with spinning and conventional tackle, as well as fly-fishing gear. We caught them with a cast net deftly thrown by mate Jose. However, the best baits and teasers for cobia would be their favorite confectionary lollipops, in the guise of the Spanish grunt. We set about to hook and line these noisy, golden, black-striped, grunting characters as well. We found a bunch of sea fans and coral heads and dropped bits of shrimp and cut ballyhoo slivers for them and hauled them up two at a time. Soon we had about twenty-four grunts, and these would be used to hopefully, if we found cobia, entice them to the surface so we could present a fly to them. The *Catch 22*'s captain went high up in the tuna tower to look for the telltale stingray that usually meant cobia. "Cobia also like to hang around pilings, wrecks, anchored boats, flotsam, etc., and will often congregate around these objects," according to *IGFA's World Record Game Fishes* book.

Cobia particularly like to follow rays; they have a symbiotic relationship with these bird-like, winged, underwater gliders of the sea. The cobia's behavior is similar to herons or hawks following behind a tractor: the birds swoop in as the hay is cut or furrows are made to eat up the mice, bugs and snakes that are kicked up by the plough or the furrow. Similarly, the ray flushes grunts and crabs out of their hiding places. Finding a ray almost ensures that there are cobias around. This day was no exception. Quickly, mate Jose threw a large grunt without a hook toward the ray and teased several cobia within casting distance of the fly-rod wielder's offering. Like cats coming to the dish, they chased the fly, and when one "took" and was hooked, the others tried to take the fly out of its mouth. It was quite a show!

The cobia is a tough customer; it fights hard, especially the large ones. They try everything to expel that hook. They dive deep and look for cutoff opportunities, so heavy leaders (sixty-pound test and up) are a must for the rough, sandpaper mouths of the fish, as well as insurance from the ravages of coral, sea fans or any possible debris that they try to free themselves on. Several cobias were hooked up, and we kept only one for the pot. They are good eating, and unfortunately, because they will bite literally to the last fish, many so-called sport fisherman take advantage and overfish them. They begin to sloppily clean them and, in the end, find freezer-burned fish that they throw away months later—what a waste! I hooked a big cobia and fought it on a Shimano Beast-Master, medium-weight saltwater conventional rod and reel. The fish was easily a seventy-pounder; it "broke me off" on the bottom after a ten-minute battle. We left the cobia after hooking and releasing several smaller fish and decided to go offshore. We found blue water after cruising through miles of the green and the gray. High above circled a frigate bird, offering the possibility of a school or single large game fish that we may or may not have been able to entice to come up and play.

If it was a single game fish that this "he-knows" (captain's colloquial for frigate bird) bird was viewing from its six-foot winged perch on a thermal, the cobia never showed itself; instead, the black fin tuna soon did. Rods were bent all around—both fly rods and conventional tackle as well. Black fin tuna don't just fight—they pull, they bulldog and are miniature powerhouses that never quit. They razzle and dazzle you. A twenty-pounder is a match for any medium-weight, saltwater tackle, but on a fly rod with a one-to-one gear ratio reel, they make the angler work for every foot of line gained. Then, in a flash, they're off again, nearly running the spool in a blazing sprint that would make the acceleration of a sports car pale by comparison. These fish put the line on the spool on the debit side, big time! They also drain the angler quickly with their power and determination. Anglers need to be fit so they can rely on their reserve strength, which means lots of sweat and hard but fun work ahead.

Often, the thrill of victory is tempered by the agony of defeat due to the black fin's habit of fighting doggedly even at the boat and then, seemingly tired, spent and ready to be brought in, the novice angler, with fly rod or spin, thinks the fish is all done-in and tightens up for the gaffer. It is then that the black fin puts on one more effort in its bid for freedom, often popping the line or pulling the hook at the moment of truth. This occurs after already thrilling the angler for twenty-five minutes of sizzling runs and a knockdown effort, which makes you feel that you'll never beat this bruiser. Of course, in the right hands, with patience and deft use of the fly rod, knowing its limitations and strengths, any black fin tuna can and, as this trip proved, will be taken. Saltwater flies that look like little squid or cigar minnows are the ticket when the fish are located and chummed up from the depths. The boat is idled, and the fly is roll cast out, jigged and stripped to entice the tuna; when one hits, it's a direct take, with fly line slithering through the guides, making an exciting, pleasing, hissing sound, and a thrilled angler bowed into a perfect parabolic bent fly rod. The black fin's colors, its streamlined, compact yet muscled body shape, is a marvel of nature. Gold-bronzed and black, they cut a stunningly pretty picture in or out of the water. They have large eyes common in the tuna family that enable them to see and hunt deep in very low light conditions, as well as on the bright surface, and they are perfectly adapted to their big-water environment. They are pelagic fish and swim the Gulf Stream based on thermoclines and their food prey migrations, which coincide with the season's natural water flows and temperature changes. Dolphins also migrate at similar seasonal fluctuations as the black fins, and very often you will find dolphins feeding right along with the tuna. Other fish such as wahoo and mako sharks, among many others, follow their food chains as well. Larger yellow fin tuna are occasionally hooked up during this

Billy Pate, co-owner of the original World Wide Sportsman in Islamorada. He was an avid seeker of tarpon on the fly rod. He was the IGFA world record holder of a tarpon caught on a fly. The fish weighed 188 pounds, and catching it was a true feat of angling expertise. He was a good friend of the author until his passing several years ago. *Courtesy of the IGFA Library, photo by author.*

time, and they are a major thrill a minute. Strong and much larger than black fin, these yellow fin tuna don't just bend the rod; they bend the angler, too. A yellow fin on a fly rod? No way! Unless it is under sixty pounds, catching a yellow fin on a fly rod is a very iffy situation.

Fly-fishing for powerful saltwater fish has to be experienced to fully understand why an angler would forsake his big stout stick to whip a fly rod for those offshore powerhouses. In Florida, there are so many different fish that you can catch on a fly rod—many of which you ordinarily wouldn't think of angling for anyway—that are a blast on a fly. Fish such as Jack crevalle, bonito, ladyfish and triple tail all give a great accounting of themselves on the end of a fly rod.

You don't have to be a Lee Wolf or a Billy Pate to be able to saltwater fly fish. A bit of practice, real practice necessary for casting in saltwater, and you can go after Pate's records, which are 188-pound tarpon, 96-pound blue marlin, 75-pound Atlantic sailfish and 150-pound Pacific sailfish, all on a fly rod. I say good luck to you, it isn't easy at all.

Going Soft on Bonefish

What brings presidents, kings and general fishing enthusiasts from around the world to Islamorada in the Florida Keys? Bonefishing!

"Quiet," said Richard Stanczyk, owner of Bud N' Mary's Fishing Marina. "Don't step on the hatch cover. Cast side arm so the bait doesn't splash too hard. Lead the fish, careful and quiet. We're getting into range."

Thus began a day in the Keys hunting for bonefish on the flat-water side of the Atlantic Ocean.

"OK, do you see where the bone is going? Cast in front of it, not too close, not too far away." The cast was made; the bait made little commotion as it lightly splashed and sunk. There was a flashing rush from a bonefish and a pickup. Frantically, slack was reeled in as the fish grabbed the shrimp, held it in its crusher-mouth, circled like a fighter pilot offering up an even larger loop of slack to pick up and then was struck. A solid no-nonsense run was the full response when the fish felt the hook—with reel drag humming to the nonstop beat of a streaking bonefish. The line commenced to melt from the reel spool as the wake made by a silver torpedo headed for anywhere but where the angler and guide stood. The rod held high to keep the line away from bottom obstructions in the form of weeds, finger sponges and anything else that could pop that slender thread between them and this speedster of the flats. According to everyone who has had a bonefish experience, the consensus is: "There is no feeling quite like that first run of a bonefish."

The bonefish looks a bit like the river sucker in fresh water. However, unlike the sucker, this is a fish that causes sweaty palms and hyper-anxiety (enjoyable to say the least) when any bonefish strikes with power far beyond

In 1939, Bill Smith was considered an early bonefish fly-fishing guide. The bonefish in this image was considered to be the first one caught on a fly. It was eight pounds and caught on regulation fly tackle. Whether this large bonefish was the first is open to conjecture, but it is commonly believed to be so. *Courtesy of IGFA.*

its looks or size. The excitement generated by these fish has caused presidents, as well as everyday citizens, to feel that they have met the ultimate game fish of the saltwater flats. Guide George Woods, who fished out of Bud N' Mary's Fishing Marina in the past, said that "the true sport instinct of anticipation in the stalk, the view of the quarry and the ultimate of fooling and conquering it for just a fleet second in my angler's recreative time out in life is what makes this fishing experience so special." To bonefish, you need a flats boat with poles, poling platforms, lightweight flats-wear clothing, a Polaroid lens that can slice any glare and a guide who knows and understands the tides. Vic Gaspeny, Islamorada guide and holder of the International Game Fish Association world record for bonefish, as well as the Florida record for fly rod–caught bonefish of fourteen pounds, six ounces, on twelve-pound test tippet leader, told me that the bonefish is his number one quarry as it is so dynamic a fighter and causes the best inshore adrenaline rush for him and his angling clients.

Former Coast Guard commander at the Islamorada, Florida Keys station James M. Henson, or "Red," as his friends call him, made that perfect cast at a bonefish. He had already heard all the stories of their famous speed, their demon runs and their drag-burning bursts. The feeding bonefish he cast to was interested. He and his guide Ken Knudssen, who guides anglers in Islamorada from his boat the *Hubba Hubba*, watched its telltale short rush and saw the splash of a bonefish on the take. First, it telegraphed a "tick tick" bite down the line to Red's wrist; he struck, and the fish put distance between them very fast. Thus began the initiation of the Coast Guard's finest to the "wonderful world of bonefishing, the flat's finest."

The power and lightning-fast run of the ten-pound silver ghost offered a thrilling challenge for the angler. Although guide Knudssen had seen it hundreds of times before, it did not diminish his excitement or the enjoyment of seeing one more bonefish prove its mettle against one more of his special anglers (all his anglers are special). The fish certainly brought Red to the threshold and beyond of another lifetime memory. Most bonefish in Keys waters, Biscayne Bay or the Bahamas are caught by casting live shrimp on a spinning rod outfit, loaded with eight- to ten-pound test monofilament line. The shrimp makes a relatively light splash compared to a jig, and its scent is easily detected by a bonefish.

If you do get a take on live bait, let the fish move off, and reel him on the line until you feel weight and movement; then, set the hook in one or two small jabs. Often, pulling like you're hooking a largemouth bass in a Bass Master tournament will pull the bait and, more importantly, the hook right out of its mouth. If your drag is set correctly at about 25 percent of line test weight and you hold your rod high to keep the angle of the line up out of the cutoffs on the bottom, you will get two or three, or more, burning runs from your bonefish. It's at the boat that most fish are lost. So if you want to get a photo before you release the fish, pay close attention to the next few sentences.

When the fish is away from the boat, you can more leisurely take your time and fight it walking slowly around the boat as it circles, giving line as it powers out and away during small bursts of energy on ever-shortening runs. But when the fish is close up, it can run under the boat, around the push pole dug in, while the guide follows you around to net or hand-land the fish. You have got to be on your toes. If the fish goes under the boat, care must—*must*—be taken to put your rod tip down and under the boat in the direction the fish has gone to keep the line from rubbing on the boat or catching on the lower unit or prop. The fish must be guided to your guide or friend you're fishing with; thus, as in fishing for any game fish, don't attempt to land a "green," mostly unspent lively fish. Also, here's a tip for handling a bonefish that Stanczyk teaches his anglers. Turn the fish on its back in the water, and it will become docile and can be handled more easily and is less likely to be harmed by jumping and crashing on the deck or the edge of the gunnel. Even the elder statesman President George Bush loves to fish for bonefish: "My favorite fish in Florida is the bonefish, and it truly is a fish to reckon with when I visit here."

According to the International Game Fish Association, the world record bonefish was caught by Brian W. Batchelor. The nineteen-pounder was caught in Zulu Land, South Africa, in 1962.

Most tournaments today in the Keys are catch and release. Photo and release has caught on big time. Olympus America, Inc. was at the forefront of bringing tournaments up to a standard that even the most jaded conservationist can stomach with its Tournament Camera Loaner Program. This program was responsible for changing dozens of tournament formats to release, as the program takes away the previous need of "hanging 'em high" for scoring and gawking. This has been replaced by viewing and reviewing photos for scoring and then allowing the tournament anglers and their guests the pleasure of seeing their day's catch photographed alive and vibrantly colored in life's brightly painted hues of gold, blue, green and gleaming silver.

Each November, the Redbone, the original giant celebrity event held at the Lorelei Restaurant and Cheeca Lodge in Islamorada, takes place. Susan Ellis, on the twenty-fifth anniversary of the Redbone Series, said the following: "When Redbone anglers started casting a line, the median age for cystic fibrosis patients like our daughter Nichole was in their early twenties. Thanks to the help of research funded by contributions to the Cystic Fibrosis Foundation, the median age is now thirty-nine—that's nearly one year of life added for every year the Redbone has existed." Just five when the Ellises, along with Gary Ellis's brother Merle, decided to dedicate a tournament to helping save her life and the lives of untold thousands of others so afflicted, Nichole, with the exception of therapy, lives a normal happy life, herself deeply involved in the tournament her parents and uncle helped start.

Merle's many talents and interests paved the way for his truly diverse career. He's succeeded in television as a double Emmy Award–winning host and director, and in print he was a nationally syndicated columnist of the *Butcher* and bestselling author of *Cutting Up in the Kitchen*. As a renowned chef, Merle also appeared on the *Dinah Shore Show* and numerous national TV talk shows. Merle Ellis called on his celebrity friends and acquaintances to help build the Redbone, Inc., Trilogy into a world-renowned tournament series. When Gary Ellis talked up on the stage about Nichole and their efforts and rewards in battling cystic fibrosis, you could see the tears well up in Merle's eyes and you knew the Redbone was one of the most important things in Merle's life, second only to his niece Nichole. Merle passed on in 2010, and he is greatly missed.

Celebrities like legend Ted Williams; John Havlicek of basketball fame; Stu Apte, world record–setting angler; Mark Sosin, fishing author and TV host; baseball's Joe DeMaggio; actor and NFLer Ed Marinaro; Dennis Harrah, retired NFLer; actor James B. Sikking (*Hill Street Blues* and *The Pelican Brief*); Channel 7's Carmel Cafiero; General Norman Schwarzkopf; Curt Gowdy; and dozens of others fished with anglers from around the world to help raise funds for the Cystic Fibrosis Foundation. At one time, director Gary Ellis even had me, as a celebrity writer and photo specialist for the Redbone, participate in the catch, photo and release scoring part of the event, with Olympus camera support equipment.

The idea for the Redbone was that anyone with the price of admission could fish with a celebrity to help raise dollars for cystic fibrosis research. One thing is for sure: this tournament has prospered and now is strung from the Keys to even Montauk, New York, and beyond. It has helped youngsters across the world live longer lives and breathe easier. This is due to the combined efforts of all those who make this tournament such a success. Millions of dollars have been raised for the foundation to use for research on this dreaded childhood disease.

Yes, the paradigm has changed today when it comes to waste and want destruction. Fishing captains and guides, most anglers and the public no longer look on large stringers and fish nailed over charter boat signs at the dock as de rigueur for sporting game fish. Fish, other than those planned for consumption, are now regularly released, even if they were game fish destined for trophy mounts. These sailfish, marlin, tarpon, bonefish and permit are now regularly sent to the taxidermists as images and not rotting corpses destined to become donations to the zoo for animal fodder. Taxidermists work with molds and fiberglass, not the arsenic-poisoned skins of game fish hides, as once was the case. Today's mounts don't begin stinking, shrinking or shriveling up with cracks as they did when the old plaster of Paris materials were used. Over the years, I imagine more than one of these mounts broke loose from a trophy wall from its sheer weight.

Chapter 11

Hemingway, Mel Fisher and Celebrity Anglers' Influences in Key West

Jimmy Buffett, the Caribe-style singer extraordinaire, has had a great influence on a burgeoning awareness of the island style of living in the Keys. First, it was grits and grunts, and now it's shrimp and grits and margaritas. The city of Key West has attracted iconic figures in all areas of the arts, Tennessee Ernie Ford and writer Ernest Hemingway among them.

The following early celebrities made regular pilgrimages to the Keys to fish and vacation: TV host Arthur Godfrey and seven different presidents, including Teddy Roosevelt, Herbert Hoover, Franklin Roosevelt, Harry Truman and John Kennedy. But none was more influential in the sportfishing arena than Ernest Hemingway and his boat, the *Pilar*. Beside penning probably the very best marlin fishing story ever, *The Old Man and the Sea* (yes, written and based on a leathered captain in Cuba), Hemingway and his entourage of admiring fishing and drinking pals held the record for turning on millions of would-be big-game anglers to the virtues of what Key West and the water surrounding this old-time wreckers-, cigar makers', turtlers', spongers', shrimpers', conch fishers' and commercial fishermen's habitat than anyone else in history.

Holding forth at Sloppy Joe's, Hemingway helped make that bar and lounge an institution. Probably no angler or any visitor to Key West passes up an opportunity to visit this haunt. Hemingway's bravado and swashbuckling for the "big ones" left an indelible mark and impression, from fishing on down to his six-toed, variably colored cats, which he had at his Key West home. He is gone, but his writings live on, and anyone for

Arthur Godfrey loved to come down to the Keys to take a break from his radio show. The popular celebrity made a point to hunt for bonefish whenever he could. *Courtesy of J. Wilkinson, president of the Keys Historical Trust.*

Hemingway and his boat *Pilar* in Key West waters were a jaunty sight as they headed out for big-game fishing. It was said that many anglers up early enough would wave to Hemingway as his boat motored past the docks in Key West. *Courtesy of J. Wilkinson, president of the Keys Historical Trust.*

Hemingway loved sail fishing, but his real love was the marlin. This image shows Hemingway back at the dock with a couple of sailfish he caught on medium tackle. *Courtesy of J. Wilkinson, president of the Keys Historical Trust.*

Hemingway, seated and relaxed, let himself be photographed for a photographer from the *Miami Herald*. *Courtesy of J. Wilkinson, president of the Keys Historical Trust.*

a few dollars can visit his Key West home and see where he penned some of his finest books and articles.

The Wrecker's Ultimate Dream or, as in Mel Fisher's Case, Nightmare

When I met Mel Fisher (he was a fisher, but mainly for treasure), we discussed markers of solar panels hooked to lights for his salvage boats. Here was a treasure-seeker/wrecker who would, in sixteen years, uncover the largest treasure in history. When the ultimate mother lode was found and itemized, I had a chance to wear the huge solid gold chain now on display at the Mel Fisher Museum in Key West. The chain was so heavy that I had to bend my neck a bit to carry it. At that time, this chain had a value in $340 per ounce, with a special collector's value of $750,000. Imagine what a gold chain that weighs more than seven pounds of pure gold is worth now?

Mel told me he'd give it all back to the sea if he could have his son back again. The whole effort wasn't worth his son, daughter-in-law or diver Rick's identification with the *Atocha*. Dirk and his wife, Angel, with diver Rick Gage, were killed when one of the salvage boats capsized. After this tragedy, any father would probably abort such a mission, but not Fisher. He had so many people relying on him, so many investors, that he persevered and finally triumphed. He told me that everything was riding on following and completing his mission—"My life now, as it was before, is absolutely defined by seeing this search through to the end. I owe it to my lost loved ones and all my men's efforts." He taught me a big lesson. In his way, he was a great man, and it had nothing to do with the treasure he found.

The following excerpt is from the *Florida Sportsman* article "Florida Shipwrecks: Fishing for History" by Michael C. Barnette:

> *For the 1622 return voyage,* Atocha *began making its return voyage in 1622, and was loaded with a cargo such as—24 tons of silver bullion in 1038 ingots, 180,00 pesos of silver coins, 582 copper ingots, 125 gold bars and discs, 350 chests of indigo, 525 bales of tobacco, 20 bronze cannon and 1,200 pounds of worked silverware! You can probably add items being smuggled to avoid taxation, and unregistered jewelry, and personal goods; a treasure that they found the hatches locked down too tight to get in. The water depth, at 55 feet, would not allow them to work to*

open her. They marked the site of her loss and moved on to rescue people and treasure from Santa Margarita *and* Nuestra Señora del Rosario, *other ships also lost in the storm. On October 5th a second hurricane came through, and further destroyed the wreck of the* Atocha. *For the next 60 years, Spanish salvagers searched for the galleon, but they never found a trace. It seemed she was gone for good. But, in 1969, Mel Fisher and his Treasure Salvors crew went on a sixteen-year quest for the treasure of the* Atocha. *They used sand-clearing prop-wash deflectors, or "mailboxes," that he invented. On July 20, 1985, Kane Fisher, captain of the salvage vessel* Dauntless, *sent a jubilant message to his father's headquarters, "Put away the charts; we've found the main pile!" At last, the wreck's "mother-lode" had been found—and the excavation of what was widely referred to as the "shipwreck of the century" began. With the treasure, and perhaps ultimately more important, were countless articles that provide insight into seventeenth-century life, especially under sail: rare navigational instruments, military armaments, native American objects, tools of various trades, ceramic vessels, galley wares, even seeds and insects. A portion of the* Atocha's *lower hull was examined and then recovered to be stored in a protected lagoon at the Florida Keys Community College, making it readily accessible to interested researchers. Following a long conservation process, many of the artifacts from the* Nuestra Señora de Atocha *and* Santa Margarita *are now on permanent display at the not-for-profit Mel Fisher Maritime Museum. Approximately 200,000 people visit the Key West museum annually to marvel at them—and applaud the triumph of the human spirit that their recovery represents. Fisher is now gone, but today, artifacts and treasures from the* Atocha *and* Margarita *form the cornerstone of the Mel Fisher Maritime Heritage Society Museum's collection. Among the items found on the wrecks are a fortune in gold, silver bars, and coins destined for the coffers of Spain; a solid gold belt and necklace set with gems; a gold chalice designed to prevent its user from being poisoned; an intricately-tooled gold plate; a gold chain that weighs more than seven pounds; a horde of contraband emeralds—including an impressive 77.76 carat uncut hexagonal crystal experts have traced to the Muzo mine in Colombia; religious and secular jewelry; and silverware.*

Chapter 12

FADs, Wrecked or Sunken Ships, Immigrant Dolphin Tactics and Mangroves

In modern times, huge decommissioned ships have been exploded and sunk to make more habitats for congregating reef fish species.

THE SHIPWRECK TRAIL

In an attempt to tame the Florida Keys and keep the reefs and any underwater features as intact as possible, the Florida Keys National Marine Sanctuary has developed ways for the public to use these special historical locations while doing as little damage to the areas as possible. So within Florida Keys National Marine Sanctuary lies a trail of historic shipwrecks, scattered along the coral reefs and buried in the sandy shallows a few miles off shore. The nine ships along this Shipwreck Trail have many tales to tell, from the stories of individuals who came before to why they were here and their difficulties in navigating these waters.

Visitors are encouraged to explore the sites along the trail. An underwater guide is available for each site on the Shipwreck Trail, providing the shipwreck and mooring buoy positions, history, a site map and information about marine life divers might encounter. Conditions on the Shipwreck Trail sites vary from easy dives in shallow water to deeper dives of one hundred feet or more, where swift currents may be encountered. Some of the deeper sites require mooring to submerged buoys. These buoys help protect the sites on the Shipwreck Trail and all the sanctuary's maritime heritage resources so that they may be enjoyed by future generations. When diving, controlling buoyancy is important since shipwreck structures can be as fragile as the marine life they support. Today, disturbance and removal of artifacts is prohibited. Everyone is encouraged to leave these pieces of history where they are for other divers to enjoy and for historians to document. With so many wrecks and so few marine patrol officers, it has been very difficult to patrol most of the areas that hold shipwrecks with more than occasional spot checks. The following information from Barnette's "Florida Shipwrecks" article offers an example of just how many shipwrecks are festooning the reefs and waters surrounding the Florida Keys:

Florida shipwrecks are more than just a productive site to pursue snapper, grouper and amberjack. A shipwreck is a time capsule—history captured in twisted steel, eroded wood and countless artifacts that can reveal important information about a former way of life. With a rich and diverse maritime history stretching back over four centuries, Florida's shipwrecks include Spanish galleons, British warships, schooners, Confederate blockade runners, steamships and German U-boats. While many of Florida's shipwrecks have been found, the vast majority still await discovery. Potentially over 5,000 shipwrecks reside off Florida's 1,200 miles of coastline. In and of itself, the Florida Keys archipelago, consisting of approximately 1,700 islands stretching 200 miles, is littered with the scattered remains of close to 1,000 shipwrecks. In fact, many of the reefs and shoals of the Florida Keys were named after various shipwreck events: the Marquesas Keys were named after the Marqués de Cadereita, commander of the ill-fated 1622 Fleet that included the famed Nuestra Señora de Atocha; *Looe Key earned its name after the 1744 wrecking of the British frigate HMS* Looe; *Carysfort Reef pays homage to the HMS* Carysfort, *which ran afoul of the reef in 1770.*

It should come as no surprise that the Florida Keys are home to countless shipwrecks. The same inviting coral reefs to which divers and fishermen flock on vacation have doomed ships large and small. Historically, vessels heading south to destinations in the Caribbean or Gulf of Mexico closely hugged the Florida reef-line to avoid the strong northward influence of the Gulf Stream. Unfortunately, all it took was a slight navigational error or violent afternoon squall to throw a sailing vessel onto the reef and tear her bottom out. The jagged coral reefs and treacherous shoals still wreak havoc on shipping today.

The most popular sites that attract divers from around the world to view include the *Adelaide Baker*, which lies in twenty feet of water four miles south-southeast of Duck Key. It was a three-masted, iron-rigged and reinforced wooden-hull bark (big hulking boat). The major features of this ship, locally known as the *Conrad* and believed to be the *Adelaide Baker*, are scattered over a square quarter-mile area. The *Amesbury* is known locally as "Alexander's Wreck." It was built as a U.S. Naval destroyer escort in 1943 and was later converted to a high-speed transport vessel. While the vessel was being towed to deep water to be sunk as an artificial reef, it grounded and broke up in a storm before it could be refloated. The *Benwood* was built in England in 1910 and sunk in 1942, when it collided with another ship. It lies between French Reef and Dixie Shoals on the bottom of a low-profile reef and sand, in depths ranging from twenty-five to forty-five feet.

The *City of Washington* wreck lies in 25 feet of water east of Key Largo; its remains lie on Elbow Reef. On July 10, 1917, while being towed by a tug, it ran aground and was a total loss within minutes. The U.S. Coast Guard cutter *Duane* lies upright on a sandy bottom in 120 feet of water one mile south of Molasses Reef off Key Largo (I was there and photographed the explosion that sent it to the bottom for the *Reporter* newspaper). After being decommissioned on August 1, 1985, as the oldest active U.S. military vessel, it was donated to the Keys Association of Dive Operators for use as an artificial reef. The *Eagle* lies on its starboard side in 110 feet of water three miles northeast of Alligator Reef Light. On the night of December 19, 1985, while waiting to be sunk as an artificial reef next to the Alexander Barge, the *Eagle* broke from its moorings. Although not confirmed, this shipwreck may be the *North America*, built in Bath, Maine, in 1833 and lost on November 25, 1842, while carrying dry goods and furniture. It lies in fourteen feet of water in the sand and grass flats north of Delta Shoals, just east of Sombrero Key Light.

The *San Pedro* was a member of the 1733 Spanish treasure fleet caught by a hurricane in the Straits of Florida. The ship sank in eighteen feet of water one mile south of Indian Key. It is the oldest shipwreck on the Shipwreck Trail, with the mystique of a Spanish treasure shipwreck to draw divers and snorkelers alike. The *Thunderbolt* was intentionally sunk on March 6, 1986, as part of the Florida Keys Artificial Reef Association project. It now lies intact and upright on a sand bottom in 120 feet of water, four miles south of Marathon and Key Colony Beach. I was at this sinking, and there were many boats out there, with most boat owners thrilled at what would become a great place to fish.

Immigrant Dolphin Tactics

The misery caused by Fidel Castro's dictatorship and the political turmoil in the Caribbean nation of Cuba has had at least one unusual benefit: the dolphin fishing season was extended an extra month in Florida.

Dolphin fishing normally quiets down in late summer months, but an influx of Cuban refugees on a flotilla of homemade rafts and boats made for a lot of floating debris up and down the South Florida coast. These floating rafts stocked with poor souls all had one thing in common: they were slow to make their way to the Keys and safety. Anything that floats attracts dolphins. Fisherman finding abandoned rafts and boats had a field day with lurking dolphins that found the cover their prey fish hang around. Cubans tie together anything that floats if they don't have a boat. A desperate situation has made for desperate measures. The shame of it was that floating humans escaping the tyranny of economic and political oppression and flocking to South Florida borne by the winds, tides and the desire to be free was the reason dolphins hung around, making for an extended fishing season for these blue-green jumping fish.

The peak period for dolphin activity in Florida has been for many years May through August. Some of the best and biggest fish have been taken in late May and June, and smaller school fish bite strongly from June through the summer months. If you can take a day cruise looking for them in the very hot sun of August, they are still around, but winds have to be blowing southeast to have better than so-so action with these fish. That year, the winds were favorable through August and September. Thus, with the raft and sailboat exodus from Cuba through the Florida Straits, anglers had an extended dolphin season along most of the coast of Florida from the Keys to past Jupiter and Stuart, Florida. Many large fish were caught hanging around discarded Cuban rafts left floating after their occupants were plucked from the sea by the U.S. Coast Guard. Dolphins have a whole lot going for them, the least of which is that they are not smart quarry needing to be sneaked up on. When dolphins are around, especially the ones known as "chicken" dolphin (large schools of young fish), anyone can catch them by putting jig or a piece of cut bait in the water. They are true suckers for anything that moves and looks like something they can chase down and eat. The blue-hued, golden green–flanked fish can chase down and eat squid, flying fish, small jacks, tuna fry and hatchling sea turtles—anything they can get their maws around.

Anyone who's fished offshore knows that if you find the weed, the Sargasso weed in particular, or anything floating in the blue or the green such as a board, piece of plywood, a barrel or even a hawser rope that fell off a freighter, it attracts dolphin. Why? Because that cover attracts small baitfish and crustaceans. So where there's food, there are predators to take advantage of the situation. The increased action was due to so much more cover than usual during the Cuban exodus toward the Keys. It's a common sight to watch dolphins greyhounding in the opposite direction your boat is moving as they make a beeline toward the trolled baits they see skipping along behind the boat. Pop goes the outrigger pins, rods bend and drags squeal and someone rushes for the rods. Once found, they are cooperative gamesters. They are found up and down the east coast of Florida, but anglers fishing in Keys waters with the easiest and closest access to these high-flying acrobats see more dolphins than anywhere else in Florida waters.

For the past year, dolphin fishing has been outstanding. Nearly every day reports have come in of fifteen- to sixty-pound (and a few larger) dolphins being captured throughout Keys waters. Most fish have been taken from 350 to 900 feet of water only a thirty-minute run from shore—eighteen to twenty-four miles into the Gulf Stream. Favored baits are ballyhoo (balao) flying fish if you can get them. A lure touted by one Marathon tackle dealer as the best in the West and the East is called the El Nacho, which throws a bubble pattern and a whole host of other plastic and rubber renditions of squid and baitfish. Colored skirts over rigged baits seem to work well, too. But I often wonder if color makes any difference. Regardless, as an angler, my preference after trying many colors over the years is black and red or green and yellow, or even blue and white. All three of these color combinations mimic baitfish colors. Dolphin, wahoo, white marlin and, yes, even blue marlin all go for these baits.

Most rigs used by novice dolphin fishermen use wire leaders, but unless a wahoo strikes, you can use monofilament leader (I like Pradco's Silver Thread due to its flexibility and abrasion resistance) in about forty- to sixty-pound test strengths. Dolphins have teeth, but they are denticles, not actually fangs or razor-sharp cutter teeth like a wahoo, kingfish or shark. They are effective, nevertheless, in biting, catching and holding anything they wish to devour. By using mono leaders, you actually will get more strikes from bigger dolphins. Big fish are more educated and are often quite finicky about how their food is presented to them. Of course, casting live pilchards or blue runners at the edge of debris and weed lines is perhaps the best way to get a strike from bruiser bulls or cows that like to lie suspended under this flotsam during the mid-day heat of tropical Florida waters. Light gear such as spinning tackle with eight- to ten-pound test for smaller fish in the three- to eight-pound range is fine. You can cast light jigs or a hook with a chunk or sliver of ballyhoo for spectacular fun. Many anglers are turning to fly tackle for dolphins as well. These anglers find it great sport to catch a jumping fish like the dolphin on fly gear. My favorite gear consists of an Orvis nine-weight graphite rod and a Fin-Nor two-fly reel, which I also use for bonefishing. For bigger fish, I have a System three-reel locked to a Fin-Nor twenty-weight fly rod that I also use for offshore billfish and tuna action. I use a forty-pound leader attached to blue and white deer hair streamers suitable for tarpon fishing, too, tied on 3/0 hooks.

Dolphins are powerful fish. A large bull dolphin may take much longer to bring to boat than, say, even a white marlin or wahoo of equal weight and longer length. Dolphins use their broad profiles and muscular shoulders to their best advantage, and they have a lot going for them when it comes to speed. It often happens that a large fish (called a "slammer" by charter captains) fights so hard that the hook wears a hole in its jaw. If you give just a bit of slack toward the end of the battle, that's when many of the big ones get off. "Gaffers," not quite slammers yet (although you do gaff slammers) are fish in the eight- to twenty-pound range, a bit too large to just haul over the gunnels by using the teeth-frayed and weakened leader alone. All slammers, if they are to be kept, need gaffing. They are just too heavy to make the trip over the gunnels any other way without them breaking loose, and they also need to be controlled so broken ankles and knees can be avoided.

As in most any other fish, dolphin fish need to be iced in fresh ice for them to taste good on the plate. The best way to clean a dolphin is to filet it after skinning. Take out that dark blood line and broil or fry small strips known as dolphin fingers. The fresh fish is so good that no masking tartar sauce should be necessary to enjoy the delicious flavor. Just a bit of key lime juice should be enough to bring out and enhance the flavor. The best side dish for dolphin is rice or baked potato. Add some coleslaw and sesame-seeded bread, and you've got a feast. Remember that dolphins grow quickly, so a ten- to twenty-four-inch fish is a baby. Try to leave the babies alone. Sure, catch a couple and then move on. Don't decimate the school. Try and find some bigger fish to fight and enjoy doing battle with.

Dolphins are not the smartest of fish; they don't live long enough out there in the blue to be educated very well, so anyone with fresh-rigged baits that can safely make it offshore can catch dolphin for dinner. However, how these baits are rigged is very important. When you rig a ballyhoo, it must ride straight and true in the water and not spin. If you put the 5/0 or 6/0 hook a bit to the side of the belly cavity instead of dead center, the rigged bait fish will spin in the water, fouling up your line and also letting every living thing that preys on a baitfish know that some dolt is after them. Spinning, unnatural baits offshore don't attract biting fish.

The best action with dolphins comes by using light tackle with jigs, but these fish tire quickly of just movement alone. So cut bait slices and chunks will keep them feeding and carousing around the boat far longer. Too often, fishermen are in a hurry to set the hook on these fish when using bait. Without just a bit of time to allow the fish to take the bait into their mouths, not just having them hold the bait in their teeth, the hook is pulled and the fish is gone. Knowledge is a party to any success in fishing, not just luck. Some knowledge mixed with sharp hooks and fish savvy can make the difference between just an accidental fish self-hooked by its exuberant strike or some continual play by the angler with several fish until he and they get tired of the game. Dolphins, especially big ones, often take just a bit of time to transfer prey from teeth to mouth. They position the fish headfirst so that their prey's sharp gills and fins fold flat and do not stab and jab their throats, gullets, stomachs and intestines. Kind of like "food fish goes in easy and out same." Knowing this, you'll hook your bait so it moves and can be taken easily and smoothly by the dolphin and then wait just a moment so the fish can properly ingest the bait. It's a surer hookup procedure, especially if you plan on keeping the fish. If you have already caught your food limit (dolphin tastes best fresh), fight 'em on a barbless jig and let them jump off at the boat themselves if that's your game. The less you handle this fish, which bleeds easily and cannot take too much abuse at the hands of the angler, the better chance the fish will have at survival.

Dolphins grow fast. A small fish has very small filets. In one year, a three-pounder can grow to fifteen or more pounds. That's a fast-growing fish! Dolphins have a relatively short life span. A fifty-pound dolphin may not be more than five years old. The easiest way to find dolphins is to look for birds; don't just "hope-troll" for these fish. Yes, they free swim, and you can catch them out of the blue, eventually running into a lone or paired set of dolphins or even a school. Boat fuel is expensive, and fish are not as ubiquitous as they once were when there were fewer commercial mother ships and anglers relying on charter boats had enough fish inshore in the olden days that they didn't have to venture too far to find all the fishing action they needed.

The best baits for trolling are Japanese feathers in from half- to three-ounce sizes, and now the newer rubber troll baits like the smaller squids and softhead lures work well. Green and yellow rubber-skirted troll baits work well for dolphins. Each year's class of fish eat younger-year class of fish of their species, as most all other fish do, such as kings, bluefish, snapper clan, et cetera. Skirted baits such as ballyhoo with red or green skirts work well on the troll. However, as mentioned above, the best way today to find and entice bigger dolphins to take bait is by running and looking for signs of fish by finding rips, color changes, working birds and, naturally, flotsam and jetsam that attract baitfish and thus their predators. When fish are spotted, casting a live bait near them is nearly a guarantee for a big fish strike. The next best shot at big fish is a whole fresh ballyhoo, or flying fish. Most rigs are wired and used by novices, but professional charter captains such as Captain Gary Starr of the *Sight Sea-'Er* charter boat, who used to fish out of Bud N' Mary's Fishing Marina in Islamorada in the Keys, cast their live baits at dolphins on monofilament leaders with 3/0 to 5/0 bait hooks. Wire is used just in case wahoos or other toothy predators hit during the troll phase of a dolphin trip, but far more live action and natural presentations to dolphins are made when only monofilament is tied between hook and line, as evidenced by noting that all professional charter captains and their mates with whom I have fished always use the mono-to-hook set-up connection.

I would be quite remiss in not describing the premier scenario for a successful dolphin-fishing trip. Head out early on a day that is not necessarily flat-calm but offers at least some chop on the water, helping to cut down on the discomfort of fishing in a no-breeze situation in tropical waters. Find working or hopefully resting birds on flotsam or locate a decent-sized drift of Sargasso weed—a weed that is actually a living floating jungle, comprising flat-leafed plants that float. Sargassam incorporates its own air-filled floats and attracts some 140 or more different organisms such as shrimp, tiny crabs and its own camouflaged fish, whose appearance mimics the leaves of the Sargasso plant. It attracts fish in the form of juvenile developing jacks, flying fish, tuna fry, tripletail and assorted sundry fish all feeding on themselves and being fed on by the tuna clan and, yes, our dolphin friends. The larger fish swarm in for the kill and feed on flying fish and anything smaller than themselves, including baby sea turtles (I recently found one just eaten by a bull dolphin and perfectly preserved right out of its stomach contents; also found were bits and pieces of Sargasso weed that was bitten off either by accident or on purpose by these voracious, recycling marauders of the deep).

Now that the Cuban government has once again cracked down on those fleeing Cuba without exit visas, there are fewer rafts being seen by offshore fishermen. But freedom's pull is strong, and many are braving, and will continue to brave, the Atlantic for a chance to reach America. Ninety long miles (by raft) from Florida, there will still be many homemade rafts and truck inner tubes drifting with the wind for dolphins to be attracted to for years to come. You can soon plan on spending some time fishing the waters off Florida for dolphins. The fish will not disappoint you!

MANGROVES MAKE NEW LAND

Often overlooked and considered by new homeowners and developers to be a nuisance plant, probably one of the most important plant species in the Florida Keys is the red mangrove. Live corals don't tolerate sediment and debris, but dead corals—the bony edges of what we call the Florida Keys today—provide conditions that allow mangroves to establish themselves. Mangroves take up where the corals leave off. The mangroves trap in their wide-spreading roots sponges and shells, seaweed and pieces of dead coral, as well as numerous other materials that wash over the reef. Mangrove roots reduce the flow of water; this further assists in enriching the buildup of sand marl and various deposits of sedimentary materials. Birds roost in the trees and drop deposits of waste. This increasingly adds fertilizer and helps increase the spread over many, many years. The islands of the Keys were first formed on the Leeward Island side of coral reefs and at the mouths of rivers where there are no corals. Mangroves are fish-aggregating flora. They naturally spread their tangle of roots. These roots offer a huge variety of species cover and shelter from predators and adverse weather, not to mention the strong tropical sun that burns fish and other species if they cannot find good cover. Virtually all fish species, and anglers, can thank the mangroves for this natural nursery. It's a nursery that allows much of their spawn to grow and establish enough to venture out as adults to procreate in their turn and get hooked as well.

Chapter 13

The Old and the New Seven-Mile Bridge and Keys Lighthouses

For many decades, locals have dropped used vehicles offshore in about fifty feet of water to attract snapper, grouper, horny Florida lobster and other more toothy species. How? They were towed on barges.

The most monumental of all building projects in the Keys was and is the Seven-Mile Bridge—the old one and the new one. Just picture running a bridge seven miles across the sea, making it sturdy enough for vehicular traffic and having it last for many decades. The first bridge was narrow and, getting on with the ravages of saltwater, it was replaced by a new wider model. It is today truly a marvel of man's ingenuity and engineering skills. The old bridge is still there. Most of it, anyway. In the movie *True Lies*, a section of the bridge actually was blown up during the filmmaking. As you ride out toward Key West from Marathon and the other islands in between, you will always see fishing boats, either trolling or anchored up to fish toward the bridge abutments and in the channels between them.

LIGHTHOUSES

Anywhere there are rocks and reefs, ultimately, as governments are pressured by commercial interests to protect commerce from the ravages of nature, they will build lighthouses if they determine that this will save commerce and the lives of sailors and passengers.

Keys lighthouses were built between 1852 and 1880. They were built of iron pilings, and their bases were driven deep into coral. From South Florida to Key West, there were wrecks just about every week, and commerce and trade required more than just the salvagers who helped make Key West the wealthiest little town. In South Florida, the Fowey Rocks Lighthouse was built; it was called the "Eyes of Miami" by locals of the day. In the Key Largo area, the Carysfort Reef Lighthouse was installed. Later on, off Islamorada and Lower Matecumbe, the Alligator Lighthouse, named after American warship SS *Alligator*, was completed. In Marathon and off the Seven-Mile Bridge out to sea, the Sombrero Lighthouse was installed, and then the tallest of all the lighthouses, the 140-foot American Shoal Light, was put in place off Cudjoe Key and six miles west of the famous snorkeling mecca of Looe Key. The Sand Key light was put in eight miles southwest of Key West. Once lighthouses were in place, the wrecker's era dropped off dramatically, except for the true treasure-hunters' searches and, as known, some fabulous finds as well.

Key West, the salvagers' dream location and some of the best fishing in the world, also had the Admiralty Court that decided to whom the spoils of the wrecks belonged and how these salvaged goods were to be divided up. The very wealthy Key West began a bit of a decline in prosperity as the wreckers' bounty began drying up. So other ways of commerce kicked in: cigar making, fishing, shrimping, turtle harvesting, sponging—all well before tourism kicked in during the 1900s. This is when Flagler's railroad and then the road from Miami began bringing in tourists to an easily accessible Keys experience.

Of particular interest to fishermen was how the imbedded legs that held up these lighthouses along the Keys began to draw fish to them. Even today, you can be sure to catch some bottom fish near the iron legs of the lighthouses, as well as near the relatively new bridge pilings (hundreds of them). Pilings offered shade and allowed fish to hide out from other predators. This cover was also provided by wrecks, reefs, the aforementioned mangroves, lighthouse legs, dumped debris, trucks and autos, refrigerators and burnt-out freezers, as well as three-hundred-year-old ships and war surplus ones exploded and purposely sunk off the Florida Keys. Bridge construction and rebuilding debris also went overboard and was a bonanza for fish habitats, too. Today, all of these locations (thousands of them) offer great diving and fishing experiences to visitors and locals alike.

Where there is cover, there are fish. The entire chain of life can be witnessed in and around these aforementioned FADs (fish aggregating devices). Fish eggs, hatched fry and various types of mollusks begin their lives on and under these areas. These, in turn, are predated on by larger and increasing larger predators and attract even the largest and most ferocious of these predators: jacks, sharks, mackerel and tuna, to name a few. Then there is man—the ultimate top predator that all fish must fear.

BRIDGE, SHORE AND CHANNEL FISHING IN THE FLORIDA KEYS

You don't necessarily need a boat to enjoy great fishing in the Florida Keys.

If you live in or travel to the Keys, you will notice boats anchored up near bridges and other near-shore structures as you travel along Florida's highways. This should clue you in on the great fishing awaiting those who fish near shore. Angling off the shores, you can find pompano, blues, snook, sharks and even mackerel. From bridges, it's snappers, sheepshead, more snook and even silver king hookups. Wading the flats, you'll find permit and bonefish. These fish can be had only with practice and cunning. From shore in the Keys, you can find the tiger of the seas, the barracuda; ladyfish; more sharks in the evening; and ocean perch, among many others in season.

Bridge fishing is really a treat. Even boat owners used to trailering their vessels often forsake that effort to try their hands off one of the (allowed) forty-three bridges that link the chain of islands known collectively as the Florida Keys. Preferred baits for bridge fishing are live shrimp, cut mullet, squid and pilchards (small herring-like silvery baitfish). The best baits in any fishing situation are live baits; shrimp are the easiest to keep alive, so they are the most popular natural bait on the bridges. Everything and everyone loves shrimp.

Just getting to and on the bridge is the beginning of your angling adventure. The important thing to remember is the time of day and tide movements, they are often critical for your success. As a rule of thumb, one hour before high tide and one hour after are the best times to fish. Even if you don't catch anything on the bridge, it's a great place to meet people and bird watch. You can view and interact with other anglers and the feathered variety, too.

Nighttime is excellent for snook and tarpon; jigs, live pinfish or mullet are superb baits for these bruisers. Snappers bite almost anytime if you do it right. Small hooks in sizes 1/0 or 2/0 and the minimum you need for sinkers or weight is the best way to go. Too many people think their lines should be festooned with all sorts of terminal tackle—wire leaders and snap swivels with heavy weights and large hooks—that bridges get an unfair reputation for being a poor place to try your angling skills. Not so; fish have eyes and good senses, so the "KISS" principle works here as anywhere else. "Keep it simple, stupid" should be your motto; make your bait presentations as natural as possible, and you will get strikes and hook fish.

Bonefish require a bit of wading, and whether using fly rod, spin or bait caster, using bait (shrimp) or jig, quiet and stealth is important. Bonefish and permit need to be stalked. They are not considered a wily game fish for nothing.

If you own or can rent a skiff or canoe, there are channels that run under those aforementioned bridges that hold all of the fish already mentioned, as well as those at certain time of the year—cobia, mackerel and other pelagic fish that usually can only be found off shore. These fish have to move through channels and waterways sometimes, don't they? Anchor up or drift with live bait such as mullet, pinfish and large shrimp or cast jigs and lures in May, June or July and you might have a large shark, barracuda or giant tarpon show up for an exciting visit. You will never forget the take of a large fish like the tarpon; it has to be experienced to fully comprehend the awesome power and thrill it offers. You'll find out for yourself why tarpon is called the silver king and remains the premier inshore sport fish in the world. It "busts" the bait; it doesn't just hit it! The bait frantically races around tethered to your hook and line; this is ultimately telegraphed through your rod butt to your hand, which will feel the surging power of a hookup with this "*Megalops atlanticus.*" (Note that your whole body and every sense you have will come alive, too.) Once attached to this prehistoric beast, you will be at one with nature and for a time feel like a kid again, totally absorbed by this moment of truth within the world's final frontier. Holding your rod in both hands, drag tight. But still with a bit of slip left on your conventional lever-drag Shimano, Shakespeare, Fin-Nor, Garcia or Penn Reel, you set the hook, which had been pre-sharpened, and then with a strong, no-nonsense pull, you ease off on the drag as your flying silver missile takes off, jumping, greyhounding and moving at "mach speed" for parts unknown. When this big fish goes airborne, bow toward the fish to give a bit of slack so his body crashes down after a jump and doesn't part the line. These tarpon put a bend in your rod like you have got Godzilla on it and then one, two, three, four spine-chilling jumps and crashing splashes, a fish shimmering and throwing green-white water everywhere—you'll think you've gone to Valhalla fishing heaven with one of these critters on.

Spoiled? You bet. Almost every other kind of fish, with the exception of billfish, will feel like yesterday's glory after tangling with a big tarpon. Just about any fish over fifteen pounds feels like a big tarpon, but remember they go into the hundred-plus pounds as well—they just don't quit. They'll take a gulp of air (only the gamey tarpon can do this), and their power restored, they will bulldog away from the boat or shore once again. The tarpon seems to be a "green" fish, even after an hour of fighting. Most other fish will finally come to the boat in less than an hour, all spent and ready for grabbing the lip with a gloved hand, but not the tarpon. It takes twice as long to get to the boat and sometimes never, after breaking you off or managing to pull or more likely throwing the hook.

Ted Williams fished with Jimmie Albright and invited the vice-president of Sears to fish with him. A huge tarpon jumped into the boat, broke the boat chairs and threw everyone overboard; with great luck, there were no broken bones. The images of this occurrence were actually photographed from another boat. I saw these images in Billy Pate's home in Islamorada. I wish I had made copies of them.

The convict-striped sheepshead is a favorite of many bridge fishermen. A bit of shrimp fished near a piling on the bridge can get you a strong, hefty one of these fish tugging at your line. What they lack in glamour, they will make up for in good eating. Don't pass up going for sheepshead; they are a fun, tough, good-eating critter.

Lots of folks I know say that keeping small 'cudas for the pot is OK—no ciguatera problems (a nerve-reactive disease caused by a toxin found in fish frequenting Florida Keys reefs). Large 'cudas seem to be the culprit, along with the bigger species of grouper and some other very large lifetime reef dwellers. I say, don't chance it, period! Throw back all 'cudas—big groupers, too—even if you catch a big one and want it mounted. Your favorite taxidermist already has the molds and doesn't need the fish at all. Take a picture and save the memories. They will safely last a lifetime. Ciguatera almost never goes away. My friend Monte Green got the nerve-damaging disease from a large grouper that he and his wife cooked and ate. They all got very ill, and Monte is still suffering the consequences several years later.

Fishing anywhere in the Keys is special; you don't have to have big bucks to try your hand at an angling adventure. A medium-priced rod and reel is all you need. Never buy junk—it's not good business sense. Take pride in your equipment and buy the best your pocketbook will allow. Throwaway tackle is throwaway the minute you buy it. It would be a shame to hook a good fish (all fish are good) only to find you have a worthless drag, bail arm or shoddy matchstick rod that a grunt can break.

Don't be penny-wise and pound-foolish. When starting out any vacation or adventure, garbage in will certainly be garbage out in no time.

So crank up the "Tin Lizzy," or today the SUV, and head for Florida's shores and bridges. Who knows, you may even catch a memory-making big-game fish like the tarpon!

Chapter 14

Outdoor Writers and a
Marathon History

The Keys are a natural venue for so many things that scream, "This is the ultimate outdoors saltwater experience!" It's no wonder many writers from all over the United States spent and continue to spend their personal, as well as professional, time photographing and writing about fishing in the Florida Keys. Outdoor editor Jim Hardie from Miami and the *Miami Herald* was one of these writers for nearly three decades, before I was offered the Florida Keys fishing editorship in 1990, when Hardie retired. Hardie was a good friend and spent as much time as he could writing wonderfully about conservation efforts involving the Everglades, the kingfish closures, boating and all things Keys. Hardie was a very thorough researcher, and his columns and articles were always spot on.

I have known Mark Sosin—a prolific, award-winning outdoor writer and photographer, as well as television, radio and video personality and past president of the largest outdoor writers organization, Outdoor Writers Association of America—for forty years, as both a friend and a go-to writer/mentor. Mark told me about his years of experience fishing and traveling the Florida Keys with his dad, Irving:

> *In 1939, the road from the mainland to Key West was finished and opened. My dad, Irv, and I drove down to Key West, fishing all the way. We stopped at bridges and walk-trolled over the bridges, hooked tarpon, king mackerel and marveled at the huge pods of bonefish by the thousands that we saw shimmering in the tropical sunlight. You could catch anything*

off these bridges, no boat necessary! When a bus or truck came along, we'd hang off the side of the bridges, hanging on by one hand and the other holding our tackle. The bridges were so narrow that you could get hit by the vehicle mirrors and killed. One thing you never did while night fishing was to stand anywhere near a road sign. "Yahoos" would drive along and shoot at the signs—an easy way to get killed down in the Keys. We fished the upside of the tide and used our old tackle so if we got hit by a big tarpon and lost the rod, it would not be so costly. I lived with Stu Apte for three months and later on in the '50s, I had a boat at that time. We fished with Lefty Kreh and Flip Pallot. We had a game going of who caught the most fish during the tide. I believe I caught four tarpon on one trip but never got as many per trip as my pals. We also played how many times on one cast we'd be hit by a tarpon as we'd get hooked up, let the line loose to let the fish get unhooked and get hit again and again by different tarpon. Whoever got the most "takes" on one cast won.

Lefty Kreh, a prolific writer from Maryland, loves the Florida Keys. He is an excellent photographer and a preeminent fly-fisher. He has authored and co-authored several books, videos and thousands of articles, many of which tell about the Keys and fishing in the Keys. Vick Dunaway, editor of *Florida Sportsman* magazine, was a regular to the Keys, and besides authoring books on fishing and cooking of fish, he found the Keys to be the place he loved best for photography and writing about his favorite subject: sportsfishing.

Herb Allen, one-time editor of the *Tampa Tribune*, befriended me, and we fished extensively in both the Everglades for bass and the Keys for snook, sea trout and whatever we could get to bite our Cotee jigs. Herb represented Cotee and was always inviting me on special fishing trips to try out new production-model jigs.

David Whitney, publisher and editor of Islamorada-based *Keys Fishing* magazine, brought me aboard for about one hundred articles on Keys fishing, but David was a crackerjack fishing writer in his own right. David loved to fish more than he liked anything else, besides eating fresh seafood and fish. I never saw David eat a hamburger—why would he? He lived just yards away from the best seafood larder in the world: the Gulf of Mexico and the Atlantic Ocean.

Sosin told me that for inshore fishing, he believes there is no finer place in the entire world than the Keys (and he has fished the world). He said, "There were fish everywhere and all over the place. There were very few guides in the late '30s and '40s, so you could pick any of the best spots to see and cast to tarpon. Today, you have to stake out your spot. Guides often go out late in the afternoon to get to their spots before they are taken; no more did you casually pick your spot." When he, his friends and his dad used the boat to find a rock pile or a wreck to fish over, they used the stopwatch method. "We used two stop watches to relocated and triangulate where a wreck was. You synchronized the watches for the time that you'd need to reach that wreck and when the times matched, you'd circle around with a depth finder to be sure you were on top of that wreck—no Loran and modern GPS then!"

The pressure on Keys fish began to build just before and right after the road to Key West was finished, as the highway and access to the Keys became easier. Sosin said that "Harry Snow was the first Key's fishing guide." Harry worked on building the road known today as the Overseas Highway. It was told that he was the man who put a spear in a seventy-five-pound permit. The fish got off. Years later, that big permit was seen with a scar where it had been hit by Harry Snow. It was believed that the bridge was Channel 2, Key Bridge.

Harry's job for the railroad was to catch fish and feed the crews working on the project. The boat he used had no motor, so he had to row to the spots where he fished. All the fish he needed were easy to catch near the docks. As the road and bridges were built, the fish retreated farther into the backcountry. He had to row farther and farther into the backcountry to obtain the fish he needed to feed the men. Eventually, to make a living after the railways were finished, he became a guide to recreational anglers. As fishing pressure increased, it became increasingly difficult to find fish in the same places he had come to depend on for them.

Beginning in 1906, for a period of more than ten years, Marathon was a railroad construction town. Activities and infrastructure relating to Marathon were centered on building the Florida East Coast Railroad's Key West Extension and especially the Seven-Mile Bridge. Henry Morrison, Flagler's engineer, created this town as the beachhead to connect the Keys to the whole world. After the job was done, the structures they left behind assisted in defining the new and second Marathon as locals and newbies began to see Marathon as a place to permanently live and to visit for fishing and other fun-in-the-sun opportunities.

Marathon became the home of one of the most celebrated fishing guides: Captain Elmo Capo. He owned a succession of big boats and took charters all over the Bahamas and around Cuba, and he knew the Keys, as they said in those days, "like the back of his hand." In 1945, Capo bought a new boat and named it *Fiji 2*. He berthed it in Boot Key Harbor. He was the winner of numerous fishing tournaments in the Bahamas (his photo hangs

Anton Topic caught this 210-pound tarpon at Channel 2 Bridge in Islamorada in the late 1950s. *Courtesy of the IGFA.*

in the Bimini Big Game Club), and he was a guide to four U.S. presidents, including President Herbert Hoover, featured in this book, and various other dignitaries and Hollywood types.

Before the Seven-Mile Bridge was finished, Marathon was the rail yard for the Knight's Dock terminal. Marathon provided sidings for passenger and freight cars and also provided a turnaround system so that trains running from Miami to the Knight's Key terminus were able to reverse their direction once they reached the end of the line. On January 22, 1908, passenger trains began running on a regular schedule from Miami to Knight's Key Dock. It took four more years before the rail line could reach Key West. The town was named by the general manager of the FEC who was a supporter of the arts and a good friend to Witter Bynner, a popular playwright of the times. Parrott invited Bynner on a trip to the Keys to plat stations for the railroad. When asked to generate a name for the station at Key Vaca (Cow Key), Bynner proposed the name Marathon, inspired by a passage by Byron: "The mountain looks on Marathon—and Marathon looks on the sea." While the "mountain" part just isn't there, Marathon actually did overlook Florida Bay.

Commercial fishermen were attracted to Marathon since the area was teeming with fish. However, there was no place to sell their catch. Once this problem was solved, and due to the fact that at that time there was no conservation laws, the decline began. It became a true free-for-all. Opportunities opened up, and it was realized that Marathon was an ideal spot to operate a fish-packing business. Several entrepreneurs came in to take advantage and built small fish house businesses at various locations, including Hog Key, Key Vaca and in the middle of Boot Key Harbor. In 1926, Paul Busby reported that there was competition among the fishermen. Busby describes occasional clashes between the "Conchs" fishermen from Key West and "Crackers," fishermen from the west coast of Florida. In one instance, the Conchs burned down a Cracker fish house. While there were commercial fishing operations in Marathon, it was not a big business, nor was it well organized, but it was just the beginning of a burgeoning trade that saw barrels of fish by the hundreds begin to roll out of the Keys.

William Allen Parrish first saw the Keys in 1912, when he took an excursion on the newly opened Florida East Coast Railway. At the time, Parrish operated a drugstore business in Dania, Florida. In 1920, he tried his hand in the commercial fishing business, generating income by buying fish from independent fisherman, packing the product on ice and selling it to the wholesale market. He began working at a fish house on Craig Key. He and his wife, Mary Evelyn Sparkman Parrish, stayed at Craig Key until 1925, when they quit the business and went to Miami. He also began negotiating with the Florida East Coast Railway to use some of the abandoned buildings in Marathon to establish a new fish business. Parrish knew from his Craig Key experience that if he could have a harbor safe from weather where he could off-load fish, ice them down and get them on a train to market,

Craig Key is no longer called Craig, Florida. This angler hung them high. No matter how many caught, most anglers, even though they had no use for the fish as food, brought them in for show. Barracuda were so common in the past that few people recognized the need for conservation. *Courtesy of J. Wilkinson, president of the Keys Historical Trust.*

he would be able to handle all the fish that the locals could catch. The abandoned railway town of Marathon had unique infrastructure left from the railway that made it the perfect town to become a major fish-processing center. Boot Key Harbor, with the old trestle, was a ready-made deep-water fishing port. The spur track from the marl trestle was perfect for a dock and provided a way to transport large quantities of fish to market. Parrish leased most of the FEC buildings as workspace and for homes for workers he would need as fish processors.

In 1927, Parrish brought his family to Marathon to start the new venture. It was a good business move. In an interview in 1951 for the *Miami Daily News*, he noted, "I leased land from the railroad on the guarantee of shipping 26 carloads a year. Instead I shipped 146 carloads a year." In addition, there were sometimes as many as ninety-two barrels in one express shipment. (Is it any wonder fishing conditions began going downhill from their former horn-of-plenty status?) He initially operated the fish house in partnership with the Miami Fish and Ice Company, which sent ice down to Parrish in freight cars. Parrish shipped back cars full of iced-down fish. In the fall of 1927 through the spring of 1928, the Parrish enterprise shipped nearly three million pounds of Spanish and king mackerel. He formed his own business as Parrish Fish Company in 1931. He continued his business through the difficult times after the 1935 hurricane and World War II and then finally disposed of the company in 1946. When Parrish came to Marathon in 1927, there were almost no permanent residents. The population grew slowly as people came to work at the fish houses.

There was only one source of income in Marathon in the early 1930s: commercial fishing. Parrish and others now had fish house infrastructure and transportation to serve a lot of commercial fishermen, and they flocked to the town. At times, there were as many as one hundred fishing vessels in Boot Key Harbor.

The highway bridges, when opened, brought a great unexpected boon to Marathon. The Seven-Mile Bridge piers had been in place for nearly thirty years, along with forty-two additional bridges up and down the Keys that were now accessible to fishermen. These bridges were and are today providing terrific structure for marine life (FADs). It is said that it was almost impossible to drop a fishing line into the water from the bridge and not catch fish. Consequently, the bridge-fishing opportunities quickly became popular fishing spots for those who did not have access to boats (most people did not). There were no regulations restricting fishing from the bridges. Tourists and locals walked westward on the Seven-Mile Bridge as far as they could carry their gear and bait and settled down for hours of fishing. They camped on the bridges, unafraid of the minimal traffic. When the tide went out, they fished the ocean side of the bridge, and when the tide came in, they crossed to the north and set their lines to the bayside.

There are tales of fishermen sitting in the bed of pickup trucks who, using long poles, trolled down the bridges while their buddies drove in low gear. Some fishermen thought nothing about stopping their cars on the bridge, getting out and dropping a line while parked on the bridge. Some locals thought it great sport to drive eighty miles per hour down the bridge, blasting their horns to scare the chum bags out of the fishermen.

News of the great bridge fishing brought tourists to the town, but the town was not really ready for them as far as overnight accommodations, restaurants and other tourist services. In 1938, there were only four rooms to rent in Marathon. Two were in Halls Camp, and the Woodburns rented a couple rooms. They were very rustic rooms in a shed that they had converted. With a growing tourist trade, there was a great need for more accommodations. The Overseas Hotel next came on line with eight fine rooms. After that, there was a small explosion in the town, as locals came down with "cabin fever." Everyone began building a cabin or two behind their businesses or on their home properties in order to accommodate the increasing number of fishermen who drove down from the mainland, stayed a night or two and then left with a hundred or more pounds of fish. By 1940, the price of a cabin had climbed to four dollars per night for mostly rustic abodes; there was still no source of fresh water, and the town had no electricity and no restaurants either.

Chapter 15

Conservation, Geologic and Archaeological Features, Sea Turtles and Sharks

FLOATING SEAWEED NOW TURKEY, CHICKEN AND HOG FEED!

Can it be that the living Sargasso weed, home to tiny fish and invertebrates on their way in their development to adulthood, is threatened? So says charter captain Dennis Bogan of the charter boat *Bogie*. Bogan says that for more than three years now, boats from Aqua-Tem in Buford, North Carolina, have taken over four hundred miles of the weed per year to sell for turkey, chicken, hog feed supplements and fertilizer. This Sargasso weed, in just one small sample alone, held 133 species of living organisms that are all part of the sea's chain of life.

The weed is actually a seagoing, organized jungle that holds embryonic and fry stages of sailfish, marlin, swordfish, several tuna species, shrimp, prey-fish food like flying fish, endangered sea turtle young and dolphins. "Take away the weed, and you may help kill much of the life in the oceans," said Bogan. The weeds circle the seas in the currents. This year, little Sargasso weed, which attracts dolphins, wahoo and all the common billfish species, has been seen offshore of the Keys (that is, until recently after Hurricane Andrew). It has been alleged that the harvesting of this weed is the cause. However, Bogan says, "the damage may have already been done. Three generations of my family since the turn of century have been involved in fishing the Atlantic. I have eleven brothers and sisters, and they tell me fishing this past year has never been worse." This damage, the taking of habitat combined with pollution and heavy commercial fishing, could sound the death knell for generations of fish to come.

Bogan's brother Raymond, an attorney in New Jersey, said that at Hoffmans Marina in Brielle, New Jersey, sport fishermen are taking the potential threat seriously. However, said Attorney Bogan, "it's not a glamorous issue, so it has had little press." Bill Campbell, owner of Aqua-Tem, said, "I harvest the Sargasso weed sixty to one hundred miles offshore in a $5 million boat, and it's not habitat for anything. We don't take much weed at all compared to New England states and the kelp farmers on the Pacific coast. They harvest more kelp in a week than I do Sargasso in a lifetime."

Randall Ramsey, president of Crystal Coast Charterboat Association in Moorehead, North Carolina, recently wrote to Roy Mahood, executive director of the South Atlantic Fisheries Management Council, asking for the council to see if real damage is occurring to the sea's ecosystem as a result of the Sargasso harvest. In a letter to the National Marine Fisheries Commission, Mahood asked if baby sea turtles protected under Section 9 of the Endangered Species Act are being killed, but so far this has not been proven (recently, Richard Moretti and Captain Tina Brown of Marathon, Florida, found two highly endangered immature Ridley turtles in Sargasso weed). However, juvenile spiny lobsters are found in Sargasso, "so the hogs, chickens and turkeys, as well as fertilized lands, are probably being fertilized with some mighty expensive and valuable marine animals," concluded Captain Dennis Bogan.

Richard Moretti and Captain Tina Brown of the Marathon Sea Turtle Hospital in Marathon, Florida, spent a year and a half investigating this issue. They helped cause the National Marine Fisheries Commission to order Aqua-Tem to have an observer on board. They told me that they were fully willing to bring suit if Mr. Mossbacher, head of the Department of Commerce, did not order observers during harvest times. However, it appears that now (and then), having observers alone is not enough. The reason is that besides turtles, the "soup" of the sea's life is being harvested—and should not be, under any circumstance—on an "I'm here first basis," or any other basis, especially when it could tip the balance of nature in a negative, far-reaching way.

Because the Sargasso habitat supports such a unique and diverse association of organisms, according to a paper done by L.C. Clements, D.E. Hoss, F.A. Cross and L.R. Settle of the National Marine Fisheries Service, NOAA, "the biomass in circulation although continually being added to from the south, which additions are part of the whole system, any 'real' loss of Sargasso, albeit only off of North Carolina, represents a loss to the whole system."

The NOAA report goes on to say that over one hundred species of invertebrates and over one hundred species of fish live in this weed. Many of them take on unusual shapes and colorations. Such specialization provides them the additional advantage of camouflage among the floating plants. The plants are definitely a nursery for many known and unknown fish. Tuna and dolphin feed heavily here, and stomach contents bear this out on inhabitants of the Sargasso habitats. Swordfish, barracudas, dolphin, triggerfish, jacks, flying fish, puffers, mackerels, billfish, wahoo, filefish, tripletail, snake mackerel, banded rudderfish, almaco jack, lesser amberjack, pilot fish, bigeye scad, blue runner, sailfish, boxfish and porcupine fish, to name a few, all closely work and live amongst and on the bounty that Sargassum provides.

When yellow fin and black fin tuna stomach contents are studied, many times Sargasso is part of the contents, conjectured to be ingested incidentally along with their normal prey. There is some evidence that larval swordfish and cobia eggs, as well as menhaden and mackerel larva, also attach themselves to rafting Sargassum near the frontal zones in the Gulf of Mexico. In addition to food and shelter, adults of some oceanic pelagic fishes use Sargassum as a substrate upon which to spawn or as a nursery area for larvae; most notable among these are the flying fish, themselves a major part of the diet of larger oceanic fishes.

During the pelagic stage, hatchling loggerhead, green, kemps ridley and hawksbill sea turtles have been observed in Sargassum in Florida, Georgia and North Carolina.

Hundreds of loggerhead hatchlings, both dead and alive, were found in a load of Sargassum deposited on the shore at Cocoa Beach, Florida, following a hurricane in September 1979. Stomach contents of the dead hatchlings showed that almost all contained Sargassum floats and leaf parts. Schwartz reported numerous loggerhead hatchlings, fifty or more per trawl, captured by M/V *My Lady* during commercial trawling operations for Sargassum. This constitutes the largest known aggregation of loggerhead hatchlings encountered off the North Carolina coast.

From the minutes of a South Atlantic Fishery Management Council Habitat and Environmental Protection Committee meeting held at Shell Island Resort Hotel on Wrightsville Beach, North Carolina, in 1990 comes the following bit of information on the Sargassum harvesting issue: Captain Tina Brown, during the public input part of the meeting, said that as a charter captain, her success usually is in direct proportion to whether she finds a weed line to troll next to or not. She knows, as the fisheries' biologists do, that Sargassum is a clear and unequivocal habitat that attracts larger predators to the vast array of living organisms that the Sargassum provides for. She felt that the committee should consider an emergency closure to harvesting weed until an environmental impact study could be done; or declare Sargassum a fishery and regulate it; or protect it under the habitat requirements for fish and endangered sea turtles. Brown was the person who presented the letter (and this article) from the Crystal Coast Charter Boat Association to the committee. Captain Brown fishes out of Marathon in the Florida Keys. A motion to have NOAA review the issue of critical habitat determination of Sargassum and advise the council within ninety days on appropriate procedures under the Magnuson Act and the Endangered Species Act was made. The motion passed without objection.

On March 1, 1991, the South Atlantic Fishery Management Council voted to develop a Fishery Management Plan for Sargassum. Bill Campbell said, "Until they tell me to stop, I'm going to continue to harvest Sargassum—it's good, rich stuff."

(Note: After this article appeared, the council did tell Bill Campbell to stop.)

GEOLOGICAL FEATURES

The geological processes that formed the reefs and the Florida Keys as we know them today began in the Pleistocene period. During this era, melting glaciers following an ice age raised sea levels to where water covered much of the Florida peninsula and all of the area that is now the Keys. The warm temperatures and shallow waters that covered this area were ideal for coral growth. Scientists have found that the Keys developed into a nearly continuous coral reef tract from the area that is now Miami to the Dry Tortugas. Core samples show massive hard corals and point to a larger, denser coral reef system than the living reef that now lies off our shores. When the last ice age struck about twenty-eight thousand years ago, sea levels dropped drastically, and the Keys, as well as the Florida Bay, were transformed into swamp and then dry land. Then, about eleven thousand years ago, water levels moderated to about where they are now, leaving the Keys exposed and filling Florida Bay. From these ancient reef formations, two types of substrate were formed: Miami oolite and Key Largo limestone.

Both of these rock types are the remnants of fossil coral ecosystems, and both are extremely porous.

ARCHAEOLOGICAL FEATURES

The Florida Keys National Marine Sanctuary's submerged cultural resources are unique, non-renewable remnants of the Key's colorful maritime and submerged prehistoric past. Submerged cultural resources are defined as those "possessing historical, cultural, archaeological, or paleontological significance, including sites, structures, districts, and objects significantly associated with or representative of earlier people, cultures, and human activities and events." The sanctuary's submerged cultural resources encompass a broad historical range from the European colonial period to the modern era. Because of the Keys' strategic location on early European shipping routes, the area's shipwrecks reflect the history of the entire period of discovery and colonization. The unique geological history of the Florida Keys, with its treacherous shallow and hidden reefs, set the stage for a colorful human history. Shoals, sand flats, storms and the coral reef itself have stymied many navigators through the centuries and taken their toll on many ships. Since the 1500s, over eight hundred documented shipwrecks have occurred around the reefs and sand flats of the Florida Keys. These vessels, which now rest on the ocean floor, carried a wide variety of cargoes throughout the centuries, cargoes that ranged from settlers, slaves and soldiers to merchandise and treasure. During the early twentieth century, the "wreckers" of the Keys salvaged virtually everything they could find, leaving behind few original wrecks. These wrecks and the stories that surround them give the Keys a rich and exciting maritime culture. In addition to the human aspect, these shipwrecks, often referred to as "windows to the past," also serve as artificial reefs, providing an anchor and abode for the brilliant and diverse life that inhabits these waters.

SEA TURTLES NEED HELP!

Marathon, Florida residents Richie Moretti and Captain Tina Brown know a lot about the disastrous results of pollution and disregard by too many people for the various species of endangered sea turtles. For more than twenty years, they have been fighting an uphill battle to save the turtles that have come to them from many sources: the marine patrol, the public and anyone who finds a sea turtle in distress. They have, with some donations and mostly their own dollars and time, set up a veterinary hospital designed to offer all manner of medical care to turtles. What they have found is that large numbers of green, loggerhead and hawksbill turtles have shown to have numerous life-threatening tumors (papilomas) on all parts of and in their bodies.

When I first went to Moretti's motel in Marathon (Hidden Harbor), I was amazed to see that what was once a saltwater swimming pool for guests was now a holding pool for turtles and numerous species of fish. The entire pool has been shade-covered and makes an excellent holding facility, shielding its residents and helping keep water temperatures from becoming unbearable for the aquatic guests at Hidden Harbor Motel.

Periodically, as the need arises, Moretti calls veterinarians from the Gainesville and Tampa areas (from locally as well, such as veterinarian Bob Foley) to perform lifesaving operations on his charges that display or are found to internally harbor tumors in or on their bodies. These papiloma tumors, which grow rapidly in many cases, can and do kill the turtles by obstructing their breathing passages or interfering with the proper workings of their internal organs and waste-elimination processes.

As discussed in the last chapter, floating seaweeds such as Sargasso, where turtles hide, feed and grow, has been, and now we find is still being, harvested (along with baby turtles) and more than 135 species of juvenile fish and crustaceans. Some commercial shrimpers (according to an NMFS spokesman, about 4 percent of fishermen) have been abusing the TED law. These Turtle Excluder Devices, built into nets, have been tampered with, modified or not used at all, taking a toll on these slow-growing, endangered animals, hundreds of which wash up on shore dead each year as a result of this wanton, wasteful abuse.

Today, and already for far too long, our seas are awash with pollutants— open sewers for all the world's garbage. In the past, these waste and sewage effluents were mostly organic and broke down naturally with time and natural bacteria. Yet today, engineered and developed chemical compounds, as well as radioactive wastes, do not quickly disappear. They remain in the environment for years, centuries and, in some cases, thousands of years. Major corporations in the United States alone are dumping both organic and chemically created cocktails of pure poison at a rate of nearly 100 million gallons a day.

Richie Moretti looks over one of his charges found in trouble by a Keys homeowner. His turtle hospital is now known around the world. Tours are offered to the public, and marine biologists come to study turtles at his hospital. *Courtesy of the author.*

"We have seen a tremendous increase in cancer rates in pets," said veterinarian Bob Foley, "and that's just the beginning. I predict more and more people will be suffering and dying from cancers caused by pollution and ingestion of plastic and chemical compounds not natural to our body's biological makeup. A very recent case I'm attempting to treat is a Boston terrier, only four years old and seriously inflicted with malignant cancer. I've been a veterinarian for thirty years and since that time tumors are showing up in more animals than ever before at an increase of five- or six-fold since I began my career." Dr. Foley, also told me that he has been cutting papiloma growths off turtles and treating them, as well as removing warts that appeared life threatening to these endangered animals, for many years. Dr. Fred Peacock, a Key Largo–based veterinarian, independently voiced the same concerns with chillingly the same mention of a five- to six-times increase in cancers in pets since his career started some thirty years ago.

So where is this increase in cancer and its manifestation in tumors coming from? Is this problem caused by what's in our water, processed foods or pesticides released into our air, ground and water, or is it in our over-and under-the-counter prescription drugs, snacks, gasses from our processed wall boards, lumber in our houses, drinking water aquifers destroyed by chemical leaching from big and small industry or radon? Often not thought of is the combustion engine and its fuel. There are many questions that will have to be addressed if there is to remain a quality of life for all of us. The diseases manifested in our wild and domestic animals are definitely a precursor for us all. Not to sound like doom and gloom—although I must confess, far too many of my friends who smoke and drank for a prolonged time have met very untimely deaths, slicing in many instances a third of their expected life spans—but I personally believe that for all the benefits we derive from mixing compounds to make lighter, cheaper, stronger materials and faster food and transportation, the balancing act is in place to put us in the deficit column in the theory that "for every action there is an equal and opposite reaction."

Yes, I feel our reefs need relief; our diminutive island shores and land do, too. So do our birds, deer, reef fish, mollusks and crustaceans. We have all heard of the tremendous degradation of our backcountry waters with blame set on several fronts—big sugar, the diversion of the natural Everglades sheet flow of water, the Army Corps of Engineers canalization of that natural water flow. At one time, there were thousands of saltwater crocodiles; today, there are only a few hundred. These saurians are fish eaters. Take away their food and habitats, and they just keep hanging on in a trickle of their former numbers. Unfortunately, it is only in recent times that the problem of high levels of potassium from upland drainage of the sugar cane growers and processors has been addressed.

The very biggest threat to the Everglades was the Army Corp of Engineers and "big sugar." In the past, it was thought that to develop Florida, the water sheet flow of the "River of Grass," as Marjorie Stoneman Douglas forever named the Everglades, had to be tamed with all manner of flowage gates, dams and other water management systems. The natural order was disturbed. However, today there is much work being done to reverse all the damage. With special water plants that absorb potassium and reopening and trying to naturalize the Kissimmee River to its former meandering, leading to Lake Okeechobee and then the Everglades, it appears there is progress being made in that direction.

Unfortunately, as the saying I saw at a Bass Pro Store emblazoned on a wall plaque says: "Remember, we all live downstream." I've stated this before and was glad to see Bass Pro, the largest tackle emporium in the world, espousing this in its stores. Well, everything and everyone lives downstream and has to rely on the good and smart intentions of everyone else upstream. All things being equal, that would be great. But, of course, they are not equal!

Thousands of types of organisms have absorbed all manner of these poisons in varying amounts and combinations, and as they are eaten and absorbed, they are then passed on to and through the chain of life by being eaten by animals higher in the food chain, along with their marinade solutions of PBS's, biphenyls, acids and caustic sodas. It is a fact that something is poisoning our marine mammals, fish and amphibians, and scientists from National Marine Fisheries Commission believe it is from phosphates from the over-subsidized sugar industry destroying the integrity of the Everglades to biphenyls from chemical companies upstream of the Gulf Stream being dumped at sea off Delaware shores.

Fortunately, marine turtles have at least one set of friends in the guise of Richard Moretti and the dedicated staff at the Marathon Turtle Hospital. As turtles feed, because their metabolisms in processing this food is slower than most other marine organisms, their bodies concentrate irritant pollutants and poisons that manifest in damage on the flippers, stomach walls, intestines and even eyes of all kinds of marine turtles. The turtle hospital deals with the effects of all this on a daily basis. The growths, many of which are not necessarily malignant, hamper the normal life expectancy of these marine animals and their daily comings and goings.

SHARKS RULE!

The IGFA World Record Book (International Game Fish Association) lists several different types of sharks in its yearly record book pages. The listings offer line class, weight and by whom the big fish was captured and killed. "Sharks are the sea's top predators," according to Mike Leech, formerly of the IGFA, located in Pompano Beach, Florida, next to the giant Bass Pro Shop "They are the sea and ocean cleaners," said Leech, or as my friend Richard Stanczyk, owner of Bud N' Mary's Fishing Marina in Islamorada in the Keys, would say, the "hit men of the sea." Anything that swims or crawls or is injured in any way or offers a weakness is an easy mark for the shark.

Sport fishermen particularly like to head offshore for one particular species known as the mako shark. This is a shark that fights like a swordfish, tastes like a swordfish and, in many ways, is even more acrobatic and tougher than a swordfish. Anyone who has tackled with a mako can tell you this is a different and awe-inspiring kind of animal altogether.

Stories abound concerning this shark. One such story from Jimmy Albright, legendary Florida Keys guide and terrific gentleman who today has his name on a fishing knot called the Albright knot. Jimmy told me:

> *We were trolling offshore of Islamorada and stopped at the Hump area* [a deep-water mountain in the Gulf Stream known as a major giant fish habitat] *and dropped a piece of barracuda down on a big-rig, giant grouper digger outfit. Before the bait got to the "hill," a big AJ* [amberjack] *grabbed it. The angler, a baseball player pal of Ted Williams* [I think it was Mickey; they all came down to the Keys to fish in those days] *bent over hard and fast to take up line and slug it out with this big amberjack. After about ten minutes, the fish seemed to have had enough and began coming up steadily without any pulling power left in it; then the rod began to bend again and the spool spun so fast it heated up the drag washers to smoking. The ballplayer reeled fast to take up slack, and then suddenly a huge mako skyrocketed just behind the stern; he had felt the hook. The big steel blue shark came down in the cockpit all five hundred plus pounds of thrashing, slashing, toothed critter and lucky for us all aboard, the fish launched itself back out of the boat in another second or two. It only ruined all the tackle, broke a favorite wooden handled gaff and knocked the mate silly without harming him too badly. If the shark would have stayed in the boat another thirty seconds, I've no doubt it would have killed us all and probably have sunk the boat in another minute more. I'll never forget that power, never. When we got back to the dock, we hung Mickey by his feet, at the weighing block; he good-naturedly took the place of the trophy fish for photos that day.*

Jimmy Albright passed away a few years back now, but when I knew him, he told all potential customers who wanted sharks' teeth that story. Most went for bonefish instead.

"For the past one hundred years or so, all around the world, sharks have a relatively new top dog to contend with: man!" According to Vin T. Sparano, author of the *Complete Outdoor Encyclopedia* and editor emeritus of *Outdoor Life* magazine, "Sharks, because they are so strong, have sharp teeth and carry a mystique about them, attract numerous two legged predators in want of their fins, teeth, liver, sandpaper-tough skin and even their flesh for food."

Legendary captain Jimmy Albright with tarpon and a customer in the 1950s. *Courtesy of Irving Eyster.*

Superstitions abound about the curative and other special powers that shark products offer if ingested. The Asian markets are full of shark fins and cartilage parts used in making soup and other concoctions.

Although there are about 250 different kinds of sharks that swim the world's sea and oceans, a relatively few of them are what are called "man-

This whale shark was thirty thousand pounds. It was claimed as the largest fish ever taken on a line. The Keys captain can be seen in its mouth. The whale shark does not have teeth; it feeds on plankton and krill. Much like the baleen whale, it sieves the ocean for its food. It is not a fish eater and certainly not a man-eater either. *Courtesy of J. Wilkinson, president of the Keys Historical Trust.*

eaters." Probably Spielberg's movie *Jaws* helped more sharks to be killed foolishly than any other single occurrence in history. This was a movie based on Peter Benchley's book made into a Hollywood fiction, and this flick scared people all around the world, making the shark, and especially the great white shark, "public enemy number one."

Benchley writes in his new book, *Shark Trouble*, "We knew so little back then, and have learned so much since, that I couldn't possibly write the same story today. I know now that the mythic monster I created was largely a fiction. I also know now, however, that the genuine animal is just as—if not even more—fascinating."

Sharks, as top predators, are the water equivalent of the land-based top predators, such as tigers, lions, leopards, polar bears and even the aquatic yet mammalian elephant seal. These animals kill and eat all manner of animals and fish as a matter of the natural order of food sources they need to survive. The same goes with sharks. To think of these magnificent animals as anything less than the perfectly adapted beasts they are would be ludicrous. However, we often hear and see sensational portrayals of these big fish that are totally fabricated. "Sharks do not patrol waters looking for people. They are looking for aquatic prey such as fish, turtles, seals, birds, et cetera. Not people!" Benchley said in an article for *National Geographic*:

> *To me the best thing is to educate kids to grow up respecting the ocean and knowing about it. If they grow up ignorant of it they will never learn the kind of respect that will preserve the ocean, and also themselves. They've got to be taught that it's the greatest wilderness on the planet, and that 80 percent of all the living things on the planet live there, and that they've got to eat. We have no entitlement to swim safely there. We're the aliens there, and we have to play by their rules. It's similar to driving a car—you don't license people to drive until they know the basics. There should be some way to educate kids to understand what they're doing when they swim in the ocean, and to understand how to take precautions against ocean conditions like tides, currents, and the like. Also to heed the hungry animals that live there. People tend to place themselves at the top of the marine food chain, as well as the terrestrial, but they're not.*

Sharks that are common in Keys waters are shovelnose, hammerhead, bull sharks, lemons and sand tigers—and that's mostly inshore. Tigers and the occasional white shark are mostly found offshore but frequently move inshore to feed as well.

The following are little-known facts about the white shark: Great white sharks can sprint through the water at speeds of 43 miles an hour (69 kilometers an hour). That's about eight and a half times as fast as the top Olympic swimmer. Scientists on the California coast tracked one shark as it swam all the way to Hawaii—2,400 miles (3,862 kilometers)—in only forty days!

Great white sharks and tiger sharks eat seals, turtles, tuna and an occasional dolphin; these sharks have also been known to swallow lots of other things. Bottles, tin cans, a straw hat, lobster traps and a cuckoo clock are among the items found inside the bellies of great white sharks. Small marker buoys, driftwood, cans and plastic bottles have been found in the bellies of tigers, not to mention people, too. My uncle Sidney still has a cat's eye gold ring that he took off a hand found in the belly of a tiger shark off his destroyer, near Manila, during World War II.

Catching shark over the gunnels. A shark fishery existed in Big Pine Key. The skins were made into shagreen, a tough, leather-like hide used in furniture, seat covers and other uses. The fins were sold to the Asian market. *Courtesy of J. Wilkinson, president of the Keys Historical Trust.*

Are white sharks man-eaters? Maybe not. Some scientists believe that great white sharks are better described as "man-biters." In more than half of all known great white attacks on swimmers, sharks have taken only a single bite before swimming away. Scientists speculate that perhaps people just don't taste as good as seals or sea lions. However, when the serrated teeth of a big shark make contact with human flesh, the effects can be devastating. Some tips on keeping you as safe as possible when entering the waters of the Keys and the entire coast of Florida: Don't swim in murky water. Don't look like bait when shark migrations are in full season (such as sitting on a surf board with hands and legs hanging off, looking like a turtle resting on the surface). Don't swim at night where sharks move in to feed (that's almost in or on every beach or channel mouth). If there are bait schools where you're swimming, get out of the water; sharks may take a bite thinking your fingers are finger mullet.

Sharks are very important to the world's oceans. Killing them for any reason except survival is foolish and goes against smart environmentalism. A camera keeps any game fish encounter alive for life. Take a picture, save the memory. It's bigger.

These results provide evidence of major changes over the last half century and a window into an earlier, less-disturbed reef fish community, but communities of coral reef fish of the Florida Keys in the 1950s were themselves not undisturbed. "Commercial fishing for reef sharks in the1930s and 1940s reduced shark populations before the 1950s, and large groupers have been commercially fished since at least the 1880s. So, like it or not, the Florida Keys are a heavily degraded ecosystem." According to Loren McClenachan, who works with Jeremy Jackson at the Scripps Institution of Oceanography in *Documenting Loss of Large Trophy Fish from the Florida Keys with Historical Photographs*, which is in press at Conservation Biology:

> *Data are sparse for most analysis into long-term population size trends. But, sport fishermen love to be photographed with their catch. Using historical photographs taken in Key West, Florida, from 1956 to 2007, McClenachan examined the mean individual size and species composition in photographs for 13 groups of recreationally caught "trophy" reef fish. The measurements show that the mean length of trophy fish has declined (91.7 cm to 42.4 cm), mean weight has also declined (19.9 kg to 2.3 kg), and the species composition has changed (large groupers and predatory fishes to snappers). The average length of sharks declined by more than 50% over 50 years. On top of that, the price for fishing trip remains the same so consumers are still paying even though the fishing is far from the good old days.*

Chapter 16

A Florida Keys Timeline and Notes about Long Key and Marathon

Approximately 100,000 years ago, the Florida Keys were living coral reefs. For at least 2,000 years, Native Americans ruled this area, but in 1513, Ponce de León discovered "Los Martires," today called the Keys. From that time through today, the Keys became settled, and the Native Americans began succumbing to diseases brought by the newcomers for which they had no immunity. Today, there are no Calusa Indians.

The first written, more in-depth account of the Florida Keys was in the 1575 memoir of d'Escalente Fontaneda titled "Respecting Florida." The history documents showed that in 1586, a party was sent from Havana to ask the Keys Indians if they had seen Sir Francis Drake. He had been sighted in the Keys area. In 1622, the Spanish treasure fleet, with galleons *Nuestra Senora de Atocha* and *Santa Margarita*, went down in a hurricane. In 1715, a giant hurricane hit the Upper Keys and cleaned house from the Matecumbe through Key Largo. In 1733, on July 13, the Spanish treasure "Plate Fleet" went down in a hurricane off the Upper Keys. Ballast stones, ship ribs and evidence of wreck working are still visible in fifteen to twenty feet of water today. As discussed, Mel Fisher and his divers found the mother lode more than three centuries later.

In 1742, the HMS *Tyger*, a British warship, wrecked in the Dry Tortugas, stranding 281 men for sixty-three days. These men suffered mightily, according to written reports about those times. The Great Hurricane hit the Keys in 1773. In 1774, the frigate *Looe* ran aground off Ramrod Key. This world-famous diving and fishing area (now off limits to fishing) is now called

Looe Reef. In 1821, John Simonton bought the island of Key West for $2,000. In 1822, the USS *Alligator* went down off the reef now bearing its name and sporting a giant iconic lighthouse. The first time the American flag flew over Key West was in 1824, when Monroe Country was established. The first settlement of Indian Key was in 1825. The first recorded duel fought in Key West took place in 1829; one participant was slightly wounded. The first Keys post office, in Key West, opened in 1831.

John J. Housman from New Jersey bought Indian Key for $5,000 and established a wrecking business. In 1832, John J. Audubon was the first tourist to visit the Keys; he stopped at Indian Key and went to Key West. In 1835, the first newspaper ads looking for tourists were printed. On September 15, a strong hurricane hit the Keys. In 1836, Indian Key (off the shores of the Upper Keys Matecumbe) became the seat of the new Dade County. In 1840, Indian Key was attacked and burned by Indians. Although John J. Housman survived the massacre on his Indian Key Island, in 1841, he died, crushed between two vessels during a salvage operation in Key West in heavy seas. In 1842, the Indian War ended, and the Fighting Florida Squadron's annual "medicinal" (liquor) expenditures of $16,000 were discovered. In 1844, hurricane-force gales struck Key West for eighteen hours, and over nine and a half inches of rain fell, basically muddying and flooding all streets in Key West for many days. In 1845, Florida became the twenty-seventh state.

In 1846, a severe hurricane hit the Keys; it destroyed Key West and the Sand Key lighthouses. In 1848, the first mail contract to a steamship was awarded to the *Isabel*. In 1849, the sponging industry was established. In the year 1852, the First Keys open-skeleton, wrought-iron lighthouse was built at Carysfort Reef, replacing the lightship anchored on the reef. In 1855, Lower Matecumbe Key was purchased for $0.75 per acre, or $613.50. (In 1995, a quarter acre on the ocean was sold for $400,000.) In 1856, one of only two clipper ships was built in the South; the *Stephen R. Mallory* was launched at Key West. In 1858, Sombrero Key Light off Key Vaca, today's Marathon, was first lit. In 186, the American Civil War began. In 1866, the Key West–Havana, Cuba telegraph line was established. In 1867, the first Key West cigar factory was established. In 1869, after serving for four years, Dr. Samuel Mudd was released from prison at Fort Jefferson, Dry Tortugas, off Key West. In 1870, the first public schools in Key West opened. In 1873, the Alligator lighthouse was built off Purple Isles, Islamorada. In 1874, the first government survey of the Florida Keys was done. In 1880, disgusted farmers were said to give up dairy farming, as cows kept falling over from the weight of the mosquitoes.

From all indications, they were being drained of blood, weakened and actually fell over dead from the swarming insects.

In 1881, Lignum Vitae Key was purchased by William A. Bethel for $170.32. In 1888, three thousand Bobolinks migrating to South America stuck the Alligator Reef Lighthouse. The sharks had a picnic! During the year 1890, Key West was the largest city in Florida. A very strong hurricane in 1893 hit the Keys. In 1898, the battleship *Maine* sailed from Key West to Havana, Cuba. "Remember the *Maine*" is still talked about today. In 1899, the first telephone was installed in Key West. In 1902, Lake Surprise was discovered by the first railroad survey party, which didn't expect a lake in the way of its railroad tracks. In 1903, Artist Winslow Homer arrived in Key West, which became the setting for several of his now world famous and very expensive art works. In 1904, the *Key West Citizen*, the only Keys daily newspaper, was established. In 1906, the Keys first radio station, built by the U.S. Navy, came on the air. On October 5 of that same year, a hurricane hit the Upper Keys and was a devastating blow to the area.

During 1908, the Flagler railroad reached Marathon Key. On October 7 of that same year, world-famous primitive artist Mario Sanchez was born in Key West. In 1909, the October 3 hurricane hit the Upper Keys. Then another hit on October 11. The Keys was then pummeled again in 1910, this time in Key West by a powerful hurricane. In 1912, Flagler's railroad was completed, and the first passenger train arrived in Key West on January 22, 1913. Also, the first flight from Key West to Cuba was made. From 1914 to 1918, World War I stimulated rapid growth of naval presence in Key West. In October 1919, a hurricane hit the Keys. A prohibition amendment passed in the 1920s, and the Keys' major industry of rumrunning was established. In 1921, James Jones was born. He wrote *From Here to Eternity* while working as a mate on a Marathon charter fishing boat. In 1926, future president Roosevelt visited the Keys on his yacht *Carioco*. In 1927, Pan American Airways was established in Key West. In 1928, La Concha Hotel, the tallest building in Key West, was built.

The first car drove into Key West on January 25, 1929. On September 2, Hemingway first visited Key West. The 1930s Depression hit. Fully 80 percent of Key West residents were on relief by mid-decade. Tourism was promoted to revive the economy. Cattle egrets, now common in the Keys, first arrived in the New World. In 1934, the construction of the Key West Aquarium was completed. Six hundred veterans were sent to Snake Creek WPA camp to build bridges and a school and quarry stone. In 1935, the "Railroad that Went to Sea" actually did in the Labor Day hurricane that hit

An image of Henry Flagler visiting the Windley Key area in 1906. He came to view the progress being made on bringing his train down through the Keys. *Courtesy of J. Wilkinson, president of the Keys Historical Trust.*

Islamorada and killed over five hundred people. Ernest Hemingway wrote of the hurricane: "We made 5 trips with provisions…nothing but dead men to eat the grub." In 1938, the Overseas Highway to Key West was completed. Railroad right of ways and bridges were used to facilitate construction. In the 1940s, Art McKee found Spanish treasure in the Upper Keys from the 1733 Plate Fleet, and for ten dollars, he took tourists out on the first glass-bottom boat to view the site. In 1942, the first water pipeline reached Key West from mainland.

In 1943, on July 18, near Islamorada, ten American sailors, the crew of navy patrol blimp K-74, participated in the only blimp-versus-submarine battle fought in any war. The blimp was downed, but not before the crew damaged the sub and forced it out of Keys waters. In 1944, the October 18 hurricane hit the Keys. The Eighteen-Mile Stretch was built from the mainland to Key Largo in 1945. On September 15, a hurricane hit the Keys. Five bombers were lost after radioing they were over the Florida Keys. This incident is still a mystery. In 1946, President Harry S Truman visited Key West for the first time. In 1947, *The Everglades: River of Grass*, by Marjory Stoneman Douglas, pioneer South Florida environmentalist, was published. On September 17, a hurricane hit the Keys. Then, on October 12, 1948, another hurricane hit the Keys. On September 22, 1949, yet another hurricane hit the Keys. In 1949, the "Pink Gold" rush hit the Keys in the form of large schools of shrimp discovered off Dry Tortugas. October 17, 1950 saw a hurricane hitting the Keys.

In the 1950s, electricity, water and better roads came to the Keys, spurring widespread development. In 1954, the first cable television system came to Key West. In Lower Matecumbe, the tollbooth ($1.00 to $4.50 per vehicle) was removed. In 1955, the Key Deer Refuge was dedicated on Big Pine Key. In 1958, restoration of historical Key West houses began with the John J. Audubon House. In 1959, the first Cuban refugees landed in the Keys. In 1960, John Pennekamp State Park was dedicated. On September 9, Hurricane Donna hit the Upper Keys. The eye crossed over Long Key, and winds were recorded at top speed of 166 miles per hour. In the early 1960s, the Beatles visited Sugarloaf Key as guests of the Papy Estate. No spiritual enlightenment was recorded. The skeleton of Jacob Housman was excavated from Indian Key the same year. The 1962 Cuban missile crisis sparked military buildup in Key West. In 1963, the *Marine Sulphur Queen*, a 425-foot freighter, disappeared with its crew of thirty-nine in the Dry Tortugas. In 1965, Hurricane Betsy's eye crossed over Tavernier, with winds recorded at 140 miles per hour. My home, bought in 1973, had eight feet of water measured in the house after that hurricane.

In 1970, the first "square groupers" were sighted on Bales Beach as drug smuggling increased in the Keys. That same year, Indian Key was purchased by the State of Florida and designated as Indian Key State Historic Site. In 1971, the first bit of treasure of the *Atocha* was found; a seven-pound gold chain often worn by Mel Fisher at his museum was also found. In 1974, the Key West Naval base closed. In 1977, the Annual Indian Key Festival originated. Also this year, Key West fire chief "Bum" Farto disappeared three days after being found guilty of drug charges. In 1979, pirates arrived at the site of Mel Fisher's find, the *Atocha*, firing at his crew.

In 1980, the Keys changed to a tourist-based economy. Jimmy Buffet was appointed chairman of Florida's "Save the Manatee" Commission. In 1980, the *Mariel* boatlift brought over 125,000 refugees to the Keys, mostly through Key West. The New Overseas Highway, with new bridges, was completed in 1981. In Key West, the temperature dropped to the lowest ever recorded: forty-one degrees Fahrenheit. In 1982, the Florida Keys seceded from the Union, becoming the Conch Republic, and surrendered to the U.S. Border Patrol at the roadblock on the Stretch (I still have my Conch license plate on my car). In 1983, two houses on Sugarloaf Key had their roofs removed by a waterspout. A Nor'wester hauled through Key Largo on Christmas Day, dropping temperatures to a record fifty-six/thirty-six degrees Fahrenheit. In 1984, the Florida Keys Wild Bird Center was established for the care, rehabilitation and release of sick and injured birds. In 1985, all taking of conch in the Keys was prohibited. The same year, Mel Fisher located the mother lode of *Nuestra Senora de Atocha*. It was big happenings and party time for treasure-salvers and investors. The State of Florida bought Windley Key Quarry and established a state park. In 1986, a thirty-two-foot sperm whale washed ashore in Islamorada. A pod of twenty-seven false killer whales beached off Key West. An abandoned pot-laden sport fisherman's vessel crashed into a Coast Guard cutter after running amok for fourteen hours in the Dry Tortugas in 1987. On October 15, 1987, Islamorada's hometown newspaper, the *Free Press*, was published by Dave Whitney (I was the fishing editor). The *Miami Herald* reported a giant, 140-pound squid caught off Ocean Reef Club, Key Largo.

In 1988, a 455-pound Great White Shark was caught off the middle Keys at the Hump. The song "Kokomo" topped the charts on the same day that the Coast Guard picked up ninety-one bales of marijuana near the Marquesas Keys. In 1989, San Pedro Underwater State Park was established about one mile south of Indian Key. In 1990, the National Marine Sanctuary was declared for most of Keys waters, and the Matecumbe Historical Board was established. In 1991, a *Key West Citizen* front-page article read, "Capt. Tony to shave his beard." In August 1992, Hurricane Andrew hit the extreme Upper Keys and virtually destroyed South Florida. I was named the official documentary photographer for Hurricane Andrew by FEMA. In 1993, Marjory Stoneman Douglas, age 102, was presented with the Medal of Freedom by President Bill Clinton, who called her "Grandmother of the Glades." In 1994, a 176-foot research vessel with twenty-one scientists aboard slammed into Looe Key Reef.

During 1996–97, sewer systems for the entire Keys were in the forefront of consideration, as environmental issues that affect the health and beauty of the Florida Keys were given high priority. Special "no fishing zones" were put into place through the National Marine Sanctuary in 1997. Islamorada considered city incorporation after receiving a huge consensus by the local residents for this to be implemented. And it was! On March 9, the *Miami Herald* reported bat sightings in the Keys and the possibility of R.C. Perky's vision of mosquito-eating bats inhabiting his Bat Tower on Sugarloaf Key finally coming true.

Notes Concerning the History of Long Key

Early Spanish charts show Long Key as Cayo Vivora, or Bivora, which meant "Viper Key," a name it kept for a long time. The Blunt chart of 1864 named it Long Island, which eventually became Long Key.

Long Key was one of the keys requested as a military reservation by the War Department in 1845. It reverted to public domain in 1879. Between 1880 and 1885, brothers Thomas and Edward Hines and Samuel Filer purchased most of the island. Large stands of coconut trees were planted on the southern end. During the days of the sailing ships, the fiber of the coconut husk made the most preferable anchor lines, as they would stretch considerably before breaking.

Construction had just started on the Long Key railway viaduct when the hurricane of 1906 struck Long Key on October 17. Principal FEC engineer William J. Krome wrote to his father:

> *At Knights Key I learned the appalling fact that one of the big quarterboats at Long Key had been swept out to sea with 150 men on board and nothing had been seen of it since. At Long Key, men had been at work on our first concrete viaduct and had an immense plant. The men had been housed in two quarterboats. These boats were big Mississippi River tie barges with houses on top of them. The barges themselves rode about 12 feet out of the water and the hulls were used as kitchens and dining-rooms.*

Immense quantities of lumber are now being shipped to Long, Knight's and Lower Matecumbe Keys, the majority of which is to be used in building living quarters for the workmen on the land. The FEC Railway had learned to respect hurricanes and to relinquish houseboats for living quarters in the hurricane season. Quarter boats continued to be used for the bridge construction crews but were evacuated during hurricanes. In an untitled November 20, 1906 newspaper clipping, we learn, "Mr. Rue is in charge of the construction from Long Key to Lower Matecumbe." The next month, on March 12, the following clipping appeared: "The greatest activity is centered at Long Key and the lower end of Upper Matecumbe Key, though there is much building and construction at other points with trains now running to Tavernier and Snake Creek. The operations at Lower Matecumbe are designed to make that a central distribution point." It appears that major construction of the Long Key viaduct was delayed until construction tracks were completed to Lower Matecumbe, which had become the central supply depot for the FEC.

On January 20, 1908, the following was noted: "At 1:30 Saturday afternoon the first engine and cars of the F.E.C. Railway in its extension to Key West, passed over the viaduct and proceeded to within a short distance of Knight's Key, which is to be the present terminal of the railroad." Knight's Key opened on February 4, 1908, with trains leaving Miami at 6:30 and 11:00 a.m. and returning from Knight's Key the next day at 5:40 and 10:00 a.m. Another newspaper clipping dated October 23, 1908, revealed: "Six buildings are being erected at Long Key for the use of tourists, and incidentally to allow the traveling public to stop over here and enjoy some of the best fishing in the world."

A *Key West Citizen* newspaper clipping dated August 5, 1909, reads: "We have tips from good authority that Long Key Fishing Camp is going to be crowded this winter. It is one of the most attractive places along the line; contains a two-story hotel and about 30 neat little cottages." Again, on February 18, 1910, the *Key West Citizen* reported: "Things are humming at the Long Key Fishing Camp. Mackerel and king fish are plentiful; so are the tourists."

"The winter vacation is now the thing. Every physician advises it. Every man and woman who can afford it takes it." So stated *Leslie's Weekly* on January 20, 1910, in regard to the Long Key Fishing Camp.

Long Key gained national prominence through its championing by author Zane Grey, who was a regular resident. Someone can check this, but I believe that Grey was America's first millionaire writer. Grey was a dentist who turned cowboy and became a prolific writer. During the winter of 1911, Grey vacationed at Long Key while writing his novel *The Light of the Western Stars*. Kingfishing was the popular sport fishing in those times, and the sailfish was considered a nuisance as it would steal the bait used for kingfish. In fact, the sailfish was dubbed "boo-hoo."

Zane Grey, along with a local fishing guide named Bill Partrea, would spend his days fishing. It is not known why Grey took to boo-hoo fishing, but he did, and on light tackle. Year after year, Grey and his brother R.C. returned to Long Key. With the support of other fishermen, sailfishing became the sport of sports for Florida Keys fishing enthusiasts. There is still a creek on Long Key known as Zane Grey Creek.

Opposite, top: Casa Marina Hotel in Key West was the first luxury hotel in the Florida Keys that catered to Key West–bound anglers and a jumping-off place to Cuba. *Courtesy of J. Wilkinson, president of the Keys Historical Trust.*

Opposite, bottom: This military general visiting the Truman's Little White House in Key West, is depicted admiring his big tarpon on one of his days off. *Courtesy of the IGFA.*

This Long Key poster was made up early in the development of the Long Key Fish Camp project. The poster claims that Zane Grey's first saltwater fish was a tarpon, and then a sailfish and wahoo. Grey fished fresh water all his life, and this was his foray in the Keys to the world of big-game, saltwater fishing. *Courtesy of J. Wilkinson, president of the Keys Historical Trust.*

Among Long Key amenities were a seventy-five-room guest hotel, a general store, a post office and fourteen cottages. Normally, a fleet of twelve fishing boats and guides was available. The two-story clubhouse and cottages were on the Atlantic side, but the boats were generally docked on the Gulf side.

Guests arrived by boat or train. A tram passed under the track to connect the two sides. The guest list included Herbert Hoover, Franklin Roosevelt, Andrew Mellon, William Hearst, Charles Kettering and other notables. Louis P. Schutt was the first manager. When L.P. became the manager of the Casa Marina Hotel in Key West, his son George took over as manager at Long Key.

The Long Key Fishing Club was officially formed, with Zane Grey as the first president from March 1917 to 1920. The stated purpose was "to Develop the Best and Finest Traits of Sport, to Restrict the Killing of Fish, to Educate the Inexperienced Angler by Helping Him, and to Promote Good Fellowship." For example, the club membership in 1929 was 133 and included President Herbert Hoover as an honorable member. Henry Fisher of New York City was the president. The season was from December 14 to April 15. The club was discontinued in 1935 and later reorganized by Del Layton in 1969.

Perhaps one of the first Upper Keys fishing tournaments began when Zane Grey presented annual gold awards. The first awards were for the longest sailfish caught on nine-thread line, the largest bonefish caught on six-thread line and to the lady who caught the largest kingfish on twelve-thread line. Zane's brother R.C. donated a rod for the largest sailfish caught over 60 pounds on a six-ounce tip and twelve-thread line. Buttons were also awarded for various catches. The list of awards grew and included bronze for tarpon over 100 pounds, silver over 130 pounds and gold over 160 pounds; bronze for sailfish over 40 pounds, silver over 55 pounds and gold for over 65 pounds. Many exacting rules and equipment limitations were in effect.

That 1935 hurricane mentioned in the Keys timeline destroyed all but the memory. A few pictures, mostly postcards, of this getaway for the rich and famous remain, but history, as time, must move on. More than five hundred people lost their lives, and many families in Islamorada were virtually wiped out, in what was considered the strongest hurricane ever in Keys history—over two-hundred-mile-per-hour winds blew away everything, including Flagler's dream railroad. The railroad is gone for all time. However, roads, airports and modern docking facilities now funnel millions to the Keys each year.

Top: President Roosevelt visiting the Keys to view the bridges being built during his administration. *Courtesy of J. Wilkinson, president of the Keys Historical Trust.*

Middle: President Nixon in the Keys to fish and golf. *Courtesy of J. Wilkinson, president of the Keys Historical Trust.*

Bottom, left: President Truman in Key West at a naval building. *Courtesy of J. Wilkinson, president of the Keys Historical Trust.*

Bottom, right: President Hoover with his bonefish. *Courtesy of J. Wilkinson, president of the Keys Historical Trust.*

Top, left: President Harry Truman on the way to go fishing. *Courtesy of J. Wilkinson, president of the Keys Historical Trust.*

Top, right: President Kennedy at Truman's Little White House. *Courtesy of J. Wilkinson, president of the Keys Historical Trust.*

Bottom, left: President Herbert Hoover fishing in Key Largo waters. *Courtesy of J. Wilkinson, president of the Keys Historical Trust.*

Bottom, right: President Herbert Hoover at the Key Largo Anglers Game Club. *Courtesy of J. Wilkinson, president of the Keys Historical Trust.*

Sources

E.K. Harry Library

Epstein, Bob. *Calypso Café*. Memphis, TN: Wimmer Publications, 1996.

———. *Forty-three Bridges to the Keys*. Taverneir, FL: Wildwater Publications, 1997.

Florida Keys Eco-Discovery Center in Key West, FL. http://floridakeys.noaa.gov/eco_discovery.html.

Florida Keys National Marine Sanctuary Final Management Plan

IGFA Fishing Hall of Fame and Museum

IGFA World Record Game Fishes Book. 2012.

Keys Historical Trust

Oppel, Frank, and Tony Meisel, eds. *Tales of Old Florida*. Secaucus, NJ: Castle Publication, 1987.

Revised Management Plan, December 2007. http://floridakeys.noaa.gov/pdfs/2007_man_plan.pdf.

Sparano, Vin T. *Complete Outdoor Encyclopedia. An Outdoor Life Book.* New York: Stackpole Books, 1972.

Strategy for Stewardship: Florida. http://floridakeys.noaa.gov/management/welcome.html.

Index

A

Adler, Alex 25
Albright, Jimmie 25, 125
Alligator Lighthouse 60, 64, 122, 152
amberjack 35
Apte, Stu 9, 25, 102, 128
artificial reefs 139
Atlantic bonito 40
Atocha 108, 112, 151, 155

B

Bahamas 16, 21, 61, 71, 100, 129, 172
ballyhoo 35, 38, 40, 46, 50, 52, 70, 95,
    115, 116, 118
barracuda 37
Bertucci, Vito 78
blackfin tuna 43, 96
bonefish 38, 124
British 61, 62, 63, 112, 151
Bud N' Mary's Fishing Marina 70, 91,
    93, 98, 100, 143
Bush, George 26, 101

C

Caloosa 55
cero mackerel 44

cigar 21, 96, 105, 122, 152
cobia 39, 94, 95
conch 13, 19, 21, 61, 64, 81, 82, 105, 156
cystic fibrosis 102

D

dacron 45
De Leòn, Ponce 55
dolphin 40, 41, 114, 116, 117

E

Eyster, Irving 55

F

FADs 29, 111, 122, 133
Fisher, Mel 105, 108, 109, 151, 155
Florida Keys National Marine
    Sanctuary 73, 74, 111, 139
France 62, 67, 172

G

Gowdy, Curt 12, 102
Grassy Key 71
grouper 18, 19, 28, 39, 41, 84, 112,
    121, 125, 144, 174

Gulf of Mexico 7, 12, 19, 29, 35, 74, 112, 137

H

Harvey, Guy 12
Havana, Cuba 62
Hemingway, Ernest 105, 154
Homestead Act 61

I

IGFA 35, 38, 41, 48, 49, 91, 94, 95, 143, 165
Indian Key 14, 55, 57, 59, 60, 61, 64, 113, 152, 155
Indians 53, 55, 57, 59, 60, 62, 63, 151, 152
Islamorada 9, 27, 35, 45, 64, 70, 76, 94, 98, 100, 101, 118, 122, 125, 128, 143, 144, 152, 154, 161, 175

J

jewfish 41, 77

K

Kennedy, John 26
Key Largo 14, 29, 32, 46, 70, 73, 74, 75, 113, 122, 138, 141, 151, 154, 172
Key lime 82, 83
Key West 13, 14, 16, 19, 29, 31, 34, 35, 39, 40, 46, 47, 59, 70, 71, 74, 77, 83, 91, 94, 105, 108, 109, 121, 122, 127, 129, 131, 149, 152, 153, 158, 160, 165, 172, 175
kingfish 45, 46, 52
Knudssen, Ken (guide) 10

L

lighthouses 121
Lignum Vitae 64, 153

M

mangroves 75, 119, 122
Marathon 9, 43, 74, 113, 115, 121, 122, 127, 129, 130, 131, 132, 133, 136, 138, 139, 140, 143, 152, 153, 172
Marine Patrol 76, 112
Matanca 63
Miami Herald 25, 26, 76, 77, 127, 156, 172
Millies Bucktails 71
Mississippi River 74, 157
mooring buoys 76
Morris, Johnny 70

P

Pate, Billy 12, 98
permit 46
Pilar 105
pompano 48, 143

R

redfish 23, 49

S

sailfish 49
sargasso (sargassum) 114, 118, 135, 136, 137, 140
seafood 16, 19, 57, 61, 81, 128
sea trout 16, 19, 53, 75, 88, 128
settlers 53, 57, 60, 61, 62, 81, 82, 139
Seven-Mile Bridge 121
sharks 31, 32, 37, 39, 40, 41, 66, 96, 123, 143, 144, 145, 147, 148, 149, 153
shellfish 55

shipwreck 111, 113
shrimp 18, 28, 39, 42, 47, 49, 53, 75,
        81, 95, 98, 100, 105, 118, 123,
        124, 125, 135, 155, 172
Schwarzkopf, General Norman 102
snapper 123
snook 49
Sosin, Mark 9, 47, 102, 127
Sparano, Vin T. 144
spears 7, 55, 65
sponges 13, 69, 75, 98, 119
Stanczyk family 10, 94, 98, 143

T

tarpon 10, 12, 16, 21, 25, 26, 28, 29,
        31, 39, 41, 46, 47, 49, 67, 88,
        91, 98, 103, 116, 123, 124, 126,
        127, 129, 161
Towe, Captain Randy 10
Truman, Harry 26, 105

U

Upper and Lower Matecumbe 55

W

Wakeman, Captain Rufus 10
Wilkinson, Jerry 9
Williams, Ted 12, 26, 67, 102, 125, 144

About the Author

To give an actual example of how and why my family and I would want to move to the Florida Keys, I am sharing my personal story. I was born in Brooklyn, New York, near the Brooklyn Navy Yard waterfront, which couldn't be fished due to the oily, polluted nature of that environment caused by commercial, navy and other workboats. At the age of eleven, I moved to Queens, New York, with my parents, younger brother and best friend, Michael. Fortunately, our home was across from Alley Pond Park, and this allowed me to sneak away and fish for warm-water species, including carp, instead of going to some of my least favorite classes. On my seventeenth birthday, I left for Israel to learn agricultural techniques, the Hebrew language and about myself, too. I left Israel after seven months, having accomplished what I set out to do, at least as far as learning a new language and learning about agricultural techniques. Finding myself would come much later. I began to and headed for Africa on an Indian steamer. I spent my eighteenth birthday on the island of Zanzibar, having traveled there from Tanganyika on a Dowh sailing craft. Upon reaching Kenya a month later, I headed for Uganda and then the Belgian Congo, where I spent many, many months photographing wildlife, meeting incredible people and fishing. I finally made it back to the United States and decided to go to Windham College in Vermont (it was next to the Connecticut River and fishing). I graduated with a BA, majoring in language arts and child psychology. I worked at a mental hospital for training in becoming a psychologist. After one year of this, I swore off that profession. A year before my graduation, my wife, Barbara, moved to Vermont. After our children came along, we moved to the Florida Keys. Barbara could no longer handle the cold-weather months, and Vermont was not an easy place to make a living. So we decided to be warm and starving rather than cold and starving. Yes, it really was that bad in Vermont for us and many others at that time. Half the state was on welfare and food stamps. I would have none of it!

As a teacher, writer and photographer, I've authored seven books on the Florida Keys, as well as a children's and child psychology book about divorce (no, I've never been divorced but see how devastating it is in and for this society). This is my first book on fishing. Our family lived in the Florida Keys for thirty years. I continued writing, fishing and diving while also traveling the world on fishing excursions and being fishing editor for the *Reporter* newspaper, the *Miami Herald* and *Scripps Treasure Coast* newspaper for several years, as well as having over two thousand freelance articles and thousands of images published in the United States, Italy, England and Japan. In 1985, I was asked to become a member of the Outdoor Writers Association of America (OWAA). Later on, I became a member of South Eastern Outdoor Press Association (SEOPA) and Florida Outdoor Writers Association (I was president in 1992). In the late 1990s, I joined the Tennessee, Kentucky, Pennsylvania and Mason-Dixon groups. Meeting with my peers over the years at conventions was an invaluable networking experience for me in my writing career. Barbara and I raised two boys. They are both moving back to the Keys since having left for careers over the past twenty years in D.C. and Fort Lauderdale. Most Keys residents are from somewhere else. They are from Cuba, the Bahamas, Canada, the East Coast, the West Coast and America's heartland, and some are from England, France, Italy, India, Japan and China. All have one thing in common: paradise found!

I was looking for paradise, so in early 1970, I piled my family into our old rusty Suburban, left my home in Vermont that was covered in three feet of snow and headed for the Florida Keys. A few days before we left Vermont, I was watching television, and Willard Scott, the weatherman on the *Today Show*, reported that on February 15, it was eighty degrees in the Florida Keys. When we left Vermont, it was twenty below. We drove 1,400 miles and reached Key Largo on February 18, 1973. Yes, we stopped at a couple of twenty-dollar-per-night motels and ate fast food all the way to the Keys while paying seventy-eight cents per gallon for gas. From Key Largo, we headed to Key West. On the way to Key West, we stopped at the Seven-Mile Grill in Marathon, where we enjoyed a couple heaping bowls of steamed shrimp in beer. We thought that the price of fifty cents per bowl (it's more than ten dollars now) was a great buy! We continued our journey to Key West—all the way peeling off our Vermont winter clothing. We were offered a wonderful room and pullout beds for our sons, David and Brian. As soon as we knew where we'd be sleeping, we headed out to the fishing docks. We really wanted to go fishing, but we had come with little cash for any special events. We walked the dog and met the captain of a party boat who offered us a special deal, not charging our boys and only charging me twenty dollars for an afternoon trip. The boat's mate provided fishing rods for all of us and baits. We were fortunate enough to catch a couple king mackerels. We were hooked on the Keys about the same way those mackerel were. We took two long fillets back to the Holiday Inn restaurant chef. At that time, they had a policy that they would cook your catch and only charge for the vegetables and drinks. We all had our first fresh fish dinner and talked about how we'd be able to move to the Florida Keys from Vermont.

We walked Duval Street and window-shopped all the tropical-style gifts and clothing. After spending a wonderful evening watching a sunset at Mallory Square and experiencing the interesting people who had varying degrees of entertainment specialties, like trained cats, a multi-jointed man who folded himself into a small box, jugglers and other fun things, we had a great night's sleep and the next morning headed back north. When we stopped for breakfast, our waitress gave us a brochure that had a discount ticket for a stay at Key Lime Bay, a newly opened time-share property. It offered two nights' stay at a luxurious condominium and a set of luggage, all in exchange for the recipient to listen to a sales pitch for buying time-share weeks. As we were virtually out of money and had no credit card to take a charge with, we headed over to Key Lime Bay in Marathon, and we were ushered into a beautiful downstairs apartment with a large deck that was cantilevered over Florida Bay. We fished for snappers and Spanish grunts, which we cooked for dinner. The whole experience was quite indelible.

The next day, we were picked up and chauffeured around in a big golf cart, and then the sales agent gave us a beautiful tour of the property. She brought us in for a continental breakfast and began her sales pitch. By this time, as a family we had made up our mind that we did not want to share time in the Keys but to move to the Keys permanently. We told the salesperson that we had no intention of purchasing time-share weeks, or months; we loved it so much, we were moving to the Keys. She worked on us anyway. However, once she realized we were resolute and adamant about moving permanently to the Keys, she backed off, and as we were the only people at Key Lime Bay, she offered us five more days in our apartment for a very small amount of money. It seems she wanted us there so when other people came they did not see an empty property. We spent the week fishing and swimming, visiting the Marathon area and having one of the best vacations of our lives. When we left, we had already decided to look closer toward the Key Largo area so that we would not be too far away from the Miami airport and the big shopping, hospitals and other services that South Miami and Miami offered. An overriding thing we noticed was that everyone we met had smiles on their faces in the Keys, and we realized everyone we met and talked to in Vermont during the winter had frowns and griped about the upcoming snowstorm. Frankly, we wanted to be where the most smiles were and where T-shirts were the rule rather than the exception. We located a rental on Tavernier Key and resolved to head back to Vermont, settle our affairs there and move back after doing yard sales and renting our home in West Brattleboro. We would move back down to God's country—the Florida Keys.

I took a waiter's position at the old Plantation Yacht Harbor restaurant. This helped bring in tips to help round out our income stream, which at that time was zero. Barb got a position with the Monroe County Building and Zoning Department. We had arrived! The first person who took me fishing in the Florida Keys was Arthur Cohan. He was a Miami firefighter who lived in the Keys. His passion for fishing was at least as great as mine. He took me in his boat to Tavernier Creek and told me that there was six-foot barracuda that would probably bite a large live bait like a big porgy or mullet. We went near the bridge over Tavernier Creek, and he let me dangle a live mullet near the bridge abutment. No kidding, here came that big barracuda. The 'cuda weighed at least sixty pounds; it slashed and struck the mullet. I hooked the fish and excitedly watched and held on tight to my rod as this powerful fish stripped the line off the reel. *Pop!* went the monofilament as it parted ways with the reel spool. Art laughed and said no one has been able to hold that fish. That fish, in a funny way, was like Moby Dick; it had hooks hanging out of its giant tooth-studded jaw from being snagged and just kept on going like the bunny in the battery commercial—but much faster!

My next trip with Art Cohan was off the entry marker to Tavernier Creek Marina on the ocean side. Someone had dropped the body of an old Volkswagen in about twenty-five feet of water. Arthur said that if we found the Volkswagen, there would be many fish of several varieties hanging around and in the car. After much searching, we found the car, and looking through a glass-faced viewing box, we saw hundreds of snappers, many grouper and other fish and lobsters. Art said that I should jump overboard and scull over the car so that he could use me as a marker to properly anchor in the right direction for our baits to be able to drift down where the fish were. I stripped down and dove overboard; I just wasn't used to wearing a bathing suit yet. My new friend moved the boat in a big circle to be able to maneuver and properly drop anchor where it needed to be for our bait and chum drift.

Meanwhile, I floated, suspended, sculling over the car full of hundreds of fish. Suddenly, a shark swam under me. I was naked and never felt more fear than at that moment. I wondered if I would be struck and held my hand over my private parts as I yelled, to no avail, for Art to come get me. I looked around in a bit of a panic and didn't see his boat and thought that he might have just left me out there to die. All sorts of things go through one's mind at a time like that. However, the reality was that the two-foot chop obscured my view, and suddenly he was there and picked me up. I scrambled into the boat as if I had been launched like shot out of cannon.

The Keys is described in many ways, by many different visitors and locals alike. There are signs that welcome visitors and also say goodbye to them as they travel the Overseas Highway, back and forth from Homestead and the mainland—signs such as "Welcome to Paradise" and "Don't Forget Your Keys." In Islamorada, you'll read, "The Sailfish Capital of the World." In Key West: "Key West & Only 90-Miles To Cuba." Actually, every island has its individual signage and flavor. But the common denominator for all of the Florida Keys is, and was for me: it can be your laid-back, world-class paradise or the outdoor Valhalla, full of tight line adventures that dreams are truly made of!

Visit us at
www.historypress.net
....
This title is also available as an e-book